900
CH
454101

Notes and Sketches
From Along The Susquehanna:

Essays in Celebration

of

American Methodism's Bicentennial

JOHN GOODELL

JOHN L. TOPOLEWSKI

Editors

Wyoming Annual Conference
THE UNITED METHODIST CHURCH
1984

Academy Books, Rutland, Vermont

ISBN 0-914960-47-4

Library of Congress Catalog Card No. 84-70504

Printed in the United States of America

PREFACE

Two hundred years into its journey our Church arrives at this generation. Will we be shoal to wreck or channel to guide the good ship on its way? Unless we know our past we will not know our reason for being—and then we will be shoal indeed.

Notes and Sketches From Along the Susquehanna is the first substantial history published in the Wyoming Conference in a full generation. It explores our roots, tells us what we have been, helps us to understand who we are, and serves as a compass to guide us toward our goal. I commend it to all our United Methodist people for reading and for study.

JOHN B. WARMAN
Bishop
Harrisburg Area
The United Methodist Church

FOREWORD

Memory, according to Reinhold Niebuhr, in his book *Faith and History*, is the "fulcrum of freedom" for humanity in history. In Niebuhr's view, the study of history, therefore, is an emanicpating force in human life. As Methodism celebrates the Bicentennial of its founding in America, historical understanding becomes a tool for seeking the freedom and deliverance of which Niebuhr speaks. While the anxicties and chaos characteristic of so much of life in the 1980's might tempt us to look toward an imagined past with longing nostalgia, God calls us to an honest—and even aggressive—appraisal of our heritage. As Niebuhr further notes, our past is present, not only in memory, but also "in the immediacy of the accomplished events which it places upon our doorsteps."

The United Methodist Church in general, and the Wyoming Annual Conference in particular, are just such "events." As Wyoming Conference Methodists, our active recollection of history helps us to discover who we are now, and how God has brought us to this place, thus opening for us the future which God graciously holds.

The title for this volume locates us geographically—we are strung along the upper reaches of the Susquehanna River—and suggests some of the reasons for our present boundaries. The essays herein raise a number of questions about our future: What, for instance, is the significance of our formative revival heritage? What does "authority" mean? What does it mean to be the church, in the latter part of the twentieth century? How are we to carry out the mission Christ gives to us? What is our Christian witness, in the face of potential destruction and/or the advancement of humankind? These questions, and others like them, concern students of Christian history; in reading, they are addressed, in this volume, to all of us, as well.

The articles that follow do not attempt to be comprehensive history. Histories of Wyoming Conference have been written, and may be again. We offer a few modest glimpses and tempting morsels, "notes and sketches," to provoke further inquiry.

The cover on this volume is a reproduction of "The Valley of Wyoming, Pennsylvania," by Jasper F. Cropsey. It is made available to us by arrangement with The Metropolitan Museum of Art, New York City.

The typeface chosen for this volume by our printer and consultant, Ed Sharp of Academy Books, is Baskerville, designed by John Baskerville (1706-1775), who was a contemporary of John Wesley.

We would like to thank the Bicentennial Committee, and other persons and agencies of the Wyoming Conference, whose support and enthusiasm helped to bring this volume to publication. We are also grateful to Nancy Topolewski for her work in preparing the manuscript for the publisher, and to Keith Beasley-Topliffe for compiling the index.

The Editors

CONTRIBUTORS

KEITH BEASLEY-TOPLIFFE received his A. B. degree from Cornell University and his M. Div. from Boston University School of Theology. His pastoral record includes service at the McClure and Pittston Charges.

JOHN GOODELL received his A. B. degree from the University of Tennessee, his M. Div. from Drew University School of Theology, and his Ph. D. from the Pennsylvania State University. His pastoral record includes service at the following appointments: in the Central Illinois Conference, the Wesley Foundation at Macomb, Illinois; in the Wyoming Conference, Bainbridge, and as Associate Pastor at Vestal, First. His monograph, *The Triumph of Moralism in New England Piety,* was published by Arno Press in 1982 as part of their series, "Dissertations in American Biography."

ROBERT W. HARRIS received his A. B. degree from Western Maryland College and his M. Div. from Wesley Theological Seminary. His pastoral record includes service at the following appointments: Faith, Philadelphia; New Berlin; Schenevus; Alderson; Greene; Lehman; Hop Bottom; Maplewood; and Susquehanna.

GEORGE S. HUNSBERGER attended Bloomfield College and Seminary, the University of Pennsylvania, the Territorial College of Guam, and American University, from which he received his B. S. and M. A. degrees. His M. Div. is from the Hartford Seminary Foundation. His pastoral record includes service at the following appointments: in the New York Annual Conference, Port Ewen, Verbank, Germantown, St. Mark's, and Grahamsville; in the Wyoming Annual Conference, Candor, and following retirement, New Berlin and Hornbrook. Mr. Hunsberger has published "The Architectural Career of George Hadfield" in *The Columbia Historical Society Papers,* and in 1968 authored *The Hunsberger Family History.*

WILLIAM B. LAWRENCE received his A. B. degree from Duke University, his M. Div. from Union Theological Seminary, New York, and his M. Phil. from Drew University. He is presently completing his work for the Ph. D. degree at Drew. His pastoral record includes service at Avoca and West Pittston. Mr. Lawrence has had material published in *Word and Witness.*

CHARLES H. LIPPY received his A. B. degree from Dickinson College, his M. Div. from Union Theological Seminary, New York, and his M. A. and Ph. D. from Princeton University. His appointments have been to teaching responsibilities at Oberlin College; Miami University, Oxford, Ohio; West Virginia Wesleyan College; and Clemson University, where he is Associate Professor of Religion. In 1981, Nelson Hall of Chicago published his monograph, *Seasonable Revolutionary: The Mind of Charles Chauncy*. In addition to being a Full Member of the Wyoming Conference, Dr. Lippy is an Affiliate Member of the South Carolina Conference.

WILLIAM W. REID received his A. B. degree from Oberlin College and his B. D. from Yale Divinity School. His pastoral record includes service at the following appointments: Camptown; Carverton; Central Church, Wilkes-Barre; and Superintendent, Wilkes-Barre District. Mr. Reid has published hymn texts and articles in *The Hymn*.

EDGAR F. SINGER received his A. B. degree from Wesleyan University and his S. T. B. from Boston University School of Theology. His pastoral record includes service at the following appointments: Associate Pastor, Christ Church, Wesleyan University; Lake Ariel; Nicholson; Providence; Honesdale; Forty Fort; First Church, Endicott; Endwell; and Superintendent, Wilkes-Barre District. Following his retirement, he has served in the capacity of Interim Pastor at Cooperstown, Mountaintop, Hawley, Clifford, and Nanticoke (New York).

GLENDA L. TAYLOR is an accomplished writer who has a number of articles and scripts to her credit. In 1978, she was the National M. S. Public Education Award Winner for her article, "With Every Step Risky: A Sense of Humor Helps." Other human interest articles and poetry have been published in *The Grit, Ford Times,* and *The Spark*. Mrs. Taylor has also written the text for "One to Grow On," a Wyoming Conference audio-visual resource.

GRACE TERWILLIGER attended the State Normal School at Oneonta, New York, after which she taught in the public school at Masonville. Mrs. Terwilliger has been active at many levels of the church's life and has served as Conference President of the United Methodist Women, and as a delegate to the 1976 General Conference in Portland. Presently, she is President of the Conference Homes Guild. She has been Woman of the Year in Sidney, New York, and was named to Who's Who of American Women. She has authored a number of plays reflecting her historical interests and involvement with women's work in the church.

JOHN L. TOPOLEWSKI received his A. A. degree from Keystone Junior College, his B. S. from State University College, Oneonta, New York, and his M. Div. and D. Min. degrees from Drew University School of Theology. His pastoral record includes service at the following appointments: Hop Bottom; Damascus; Lanesboro; Associate Pastor, First Church, Oneonta; Trucksville; and Mountaintop. Dr. Topolewski has had a number of articles, reviews, and sermons published in *Clergy Journal, The Drew Gateway, Homiletic, Insights, Nexus, Quarterly Review, Thanatos,* and *Word and Witness.* He serves on the Editorial Board of *Quarterly Review* and is a member of the Advisory Committee on United Methodist Studies, which produced *United Methodist Studies: Basic Bibliographies.*

WITH DEEP THANKSGIVING: WYOMING'S HISTORIANS

John L. Topolewski

In the year 1909, William P. Merrill, Pastor of the Sixth Avenue Presbyterian Church in Chicago, attended a Union Thanksgiving Service, at which he was deeply moved by the prayer. Offered by Jenkin Lloyd Jones, the prayer invoked images of blessings and assets which were spiritual in nature. In response, Merrill wrote the hymn, "Not Alone for Mighty Empire." It was first published in 1911, was included in the Methodist Hymnal of 1935, and stands as #548 in our present *Book of Hymns*.[1]

The closing couplet of the first verse of Merrill's hymn contains an idea which, I am sure, is never far from the heart and mind of the church historian, or, for that matter, of many students of social and intellectual history:

> *Standing in the living present,*
> *Memory and hope between,*
> *Lord, we would with deep thanksgiving*
> *Praise thee most for things unseen.*

The historical task is often to discover those data, those events or combinations of events, which, taken together, have altered the lives of many. An institutional historian is even more restricted, as there is actually a physical or corporate entity or entities which can be researched, evaluated, and reported upon. But there is more to history than bricks and mortar, facts and dates, events and names. Real history takes into account "things unseen": faith and dreams, hopes and aspirations, anxieties and fears, a myriad of motivations which call physical, definable history into being. It is possible to speak of the history of the Wyoming Annual Conference in factual terms only, but to do so would be to commit a grave injustice. This Conference, our Conference, grows out of the lives and faith, the commitment and sacrifices of untold, and often unrecalled, women, children, and men who made it possible.

This essay is a brief tribute to four individuals, who share the distinction of having published, in book form, their histories of our Conference: George Peck, Amasa Franklin Chaffee, Louis D. Palmer, and Leroy E. Bugbee. We are beneficiaries of their legacy, for they stood between memory and hope, giving witness to things seen, and thanksgiving for things unseen.

GEORGE PECK (1797-1876)

When considering both the makers and the writers of Wyoming's history, one individual stands head and shoulders above the rest. George

Peck, pastor, administrator, editor, legislator, and historian, remains, even today, the most prominent and eminent Conference member in our history. His life and work are crucial to any attempt to understand the growth and development of Methodism in this area, and his presence and influence within those circles of the national church in which the most significant transitions of the mid-nineteenth century were executed, was most formidable.

In that other authors in this volume of essays will speak of Peck, and one essay will be entirely devoted to him, I will not attempt to duplicate their work. Instead, let us look to a contemporary of Peck's, Bishop Matthew Simpson, himself a formidable nineteenth-century Methodist personage, for a brief biographical sketch:

> *Peck, George, D. D.*, a distinguished minister of the M. E. Church, was born in Middlefield, Otsego Co., N. Y., Aug. 8, 1797. His mother was an amiable woman, eminently pious and devotional, and gave five sons to the Methodist ministry. He united with the church in 1812, and in 1816, at the age of nineteen, entered the ministry. Studious, diligent, and successful, he was, in 1824, appointed presiding elder of the Susquehanna district, then containing all the territory of the Wyoming Conference as constituted in 1868 [sic], and as much more in the New York and Genessee Conferences. He was a member of every General Conference from 1824 to 1872. In 1835 he was elected principal of the Oneida Conference Seminary. Though peculiarly adapted to the education of the young, after four years he returned to the active duties of the ministry, and was again appointed presiding elder of the Susquehanna district. In 1840 he was elected editor of *The Methodist Quarterly Review,* which position he filled for eight years; and in 1848 he was elected editor of *The Christian Advocate,* where he remained for four years. He was also delegate to the first Evangelical Alliance in London, and took a leading part in its deliberations. Returning to the pastorate in 1852, he filled some of the most important appointments in his Conference, and was also presiding elder of the Lackawanna and Wyoming districts. He was superannuated in 1873, and died May 20, 1876.[1]

Amasa Chaffee provides us with a more detailed record of Peck's itineracy:

> The following were his fields of labor: 1816, Broome (junior preacher); 1817, Cortland (junior preacher); 1818, Wyoming; 1819, Bridgewater; 1820, Canaan; 1821, Paris; 1822-23, Utica; 1824-25, Presiding Elder of Susquehanna District; 1826, Wyoming; 1827, Wilkes-Barre; 1828-29, Ithaca; 1830, Utica; 1831-32, Cazenovia; 1833-34, Auburn; 1835-38, Principal of Cazenovia Seminary; 1839, Presiding Elder of Susquehanna District; 1840-47, Editor of the *Methodist Quarterly Review* and general Book Editor of the Book Concern; 1848-51, editor of *The Christian Advocate;* 1852-53, Wilkes-Barre; 1854, Presiding Elder of Wyoming District; 1855, Presiding Elder of Binghamton District; 1856-57, Scranton Mission (Elm Park); 1858-61, Presiding Elder of Wyoming District; 1862-65, Presiding Elder of Lackawanna District; 1866-67, Providence; 1868, Dunmore; 1869-72, Presiding Elder of Wyoming District; 1873-76, sd.[2]

Of his many publications, I wish to comment briefly upon those three volumes of special interest to students of our Conference's history: *Wyoming: Its History, Stirring Incidents, and Romantic Adventures* (1860); *Early Methodism Within the Bounds of the Old Genessee Conference From 1788-1828* (1860); and *The Life and Times of George Peck, D. D.* (1874).

Wyoming, completed at Scranton in April of 1858, is a collection of stories and folk history, which emerged out of the Wyoming Valley. More than a quarter of the volume is given over to the story of the Wyoming

Massacre, the escape of Anning Owen and the capture of Frances Slocum. In some cases, the materials collected have been passed directly to the author and are valued source material. But, in many ways, the work is a romance, and is transparent to the values and prejudices of that pioneer stock, who, at some risk, settled the Valley and provided the base out of which the church would grow. Peck's comments on Native Americans supply revealing commentary upon the time in which he wrote this work:

> Making captives, particularly of children, and adopting them as their own, is one of the laws of Indian warfare. Usually the little captive is adopted by a mother who has lost a child. If a son is lost in battle, or a daughter perishes by hunger or fatigue, or dies by disease, the vacancy, if possible, is supplied by some palefaced prisoner, who is imagined to bear some distant resemblance to the lost one. . . . But it is probable that the main ground for this species of plunder is part of a system of *cruel vengeance,* with which the savage heart delights to glut itself for real or supposed wrongs.[3]

Early Methodism, completed in Scranton in March of 1860, is a rich treasure of primary materials focusing upon the early leaders of the Methodist movement, the deployment of preachers, the formation and development of circuits, and an overview of what was then commonly referred to as "the work." In many ways, it is the best of the three historical volumes, and one of its principal strengths lies in its ability to recognize the universal within the particular. Peck states it in these words:

> Methodism is one of the great facts of modern civilization, and its vital elements are brought out in its practical results, and particularly in the examples of its actors, great and small. The history of Methodism in one age or place is its history in all ages and places, with the exception of the slight variation which is effected by time.[4]

The autobiographical *Life and Times* is of special interest and value to those who wish to explore Peck's involvement within the life of the national church. Peck was very much a part of the conflict within the church over Bishop James O. Andrew, a slaveholder—a conflict which was but symptomatic of a larger division between the church, north and south. He saw the conflict, as it surfaced at the General Conference of 1844, as irreconcilable.

> To do what the Southern members deemed essential to the welfare of the Churches in their section would ruin whole Conferences at the North; and even to temporize was full of peril. To do all that Northern sentiment demanded, would have torn the Southern Conferences to shreds.[5]

Arthur Jones, of Drew University, documents Peck's involvement in the handling of the crises and the division of the church, which was its outcome, and supplements Peck's personal reflections and remembrances.[6]

Peck's work as Editor of both *Quarterly Review* and *The Christian Advocate* is detailed, and a refreshing travelogue concerning his journey to Europe is included in *Life and Times.* As in *Early Methodism,* significant attention is given to the early circuits, and, in this volume, the role he played in their development.

In 1873, George Peck entered into the superannuated relationship. The Wyoming Conference was in session at Waverley, New York, and at seventy-five years of age, and after fifty-seven years of service, George Peck would reflect upon his life and work in words that were typically direct, and uncharacteristically spare: "I bless him for the past, and, with unfaltering trust, look forward to the future."[7]

Any attempt to understand our history as a Conference must, of necessity, be initially dependent upon George Peck, and forever in his debt.

AMASA FRANKLIN CHAFFEE (1855-1926)

There are two published references to the life and work of Amasa Franklin Chaffee. The first is autobiographical and appears in the section on "Living Preachers" within his own *History of the Wyoming Conference*. The second was written almost five decades later, by Leroy E. Bugbee, and opens Chapter IX, "Men and Movements," in his centennial history, *He Holds the Stars in His Hands*.

Because Chaffee's statement is, in itself, reflective and representative of the style and structure employed throughout his work, and because it is so obviously representative of what he wanted others to know about him, I have chosen to include it here in its entirety:

CHAFFEE, AMASA FRANKLIN, was born on February 22, 1855, in Dayton, Cattaraugus County, N. Y. He attended the village schools in the various towns where the family lived until they moved to Randolph, N. Y. Here he entered Chamberlain Institute, the Conference seminary of Erie Conference, and prepared for college. While his father offered to send him to college, he became convinced that such was not his father's desire, and therefore turned his attention in other directions. In the winter of 1872, while he was teaching the village school at Napoli, N. Y., he was converted. One of the prime factors in bringing him to a decision was the reading of Holland's *Bitter Sweet*. In the spring of 1873, after his winter's work in teaching was over, he went to Jamestown, N. Y., where his family had moved in the preceeding November. Here he entered the employ of a hardware merchant, he having considerable knowledge of that business, his father having been a hardware merchant for years. In 1875 he went to Gowanda, N. Y., and established a fire and life insurance agency.

The summer of 1877 saw the ripening and completion of years of thought concerning his lifework. Shortly after his going to Jamestown he united with the Church. Active work in the Church prompted the Church to urge the ministry as a lifework. Some time prior to this he had heard God's voice calling. This was stubbornly resisted for some years, as his training and taste inclined him to business. In June of 1877 he settled the question, sold his agency, and turned his face toward the ministry. During two and a half years he had pursued studies in the college course, thinking that perhaps some day he might gratify his desire for a collegiate course of study. Upon the advice of his cousin, Dr. L. H. Bugbee, president of Allegheny College, he entered Drew Theological Seminary, expecting to finish the college course at some later day. He paid his way through the theological seminary one year by printing Dr. Strong's lectures on Old Testament history, and the other three years by preaching. He graduated in 1881, the last year of his work at Drew being almost wholly post-graduate. In 1882 he joined Wyoming Conference, at the suggestion of Bishop Hurst. Since entering the Conference he has completed his college course. From these schools he has Ph.B. and B.D.

He was licensed as a local preacher in the fall of 1877 and 1878 by the Jamestown church, and the subsequent renewals were by the churches in New Jersey which he supplied.

On October 20, 1881, he married Miss Maria Ann Manners, of Milburn, N. J.

His pastoral record is as follows: 1882, Laurens; 1883-84, Afton; 1885-87, Cooperstown; 1888-92, Union; 1893, Derr Memorial, Wilkes-Barre; 1894-98, Asbury, Scranton; 1899-1903, Carbondale.[1]

The volume itself was completed at Carbondale on 10 December 1903, and published the following year. As an addendum to his Pastoral Record cited above, Chaffee served at Owego during the 1904 Conference year, and for a small portion of 1905, as well.[2]

In addition to producing his exhaustive work of Conference history, Chaffee left a second legacy to Wyoming. In 1900 he proposed that substantial changes be made in the number and geographical boundaries of the six Districts of the Conference. Chaffee was appointed to chair a commission which would return with a recommendation to the Conference of 1901. The report called for the creation of five Districts. However, due to a strong and vocal minority, in opposition to restructuring, the Bishop postponed action. It would not be until 1909-1910 that a decision would be reached, and even then, not without strong disagreement, to redistrict the Conference into four units.[3] With only minor modifications, the units and boundaries created in 1910 remain in place today.

For reasons no longer known, A. F. Chaffee left Owego and the Wyoming Conference, transferring to the Colorado Conference in 1905. His record of service there includes: 1905-1906, Canon City, Colorado; 1907-1908, Christ Church, Denver.[4] In 1909 Chaffee again transferred, this time to Kansas, where he served at Independence, 1909-1912. At Conference in 1913, he retired, and at some point returned to Colorado, where, thirteen years later, on 16 May 1926, he died in the town of Hotchkiss. His body was returned to the East and was buried in Scranton, Pennsylvania.[5]

Chaffee's volume of Conference history represents a most unique undertaking. Of this work, Bugbee would write, "The reader is still amazed by the mass of factual details he had collected and the interest he had infused into the material. There are close to a thousand pages which represent seven or eight years of gathering information, while he fulfilled the duties of a regular charge."[6] Divided into seventeen chapters, the work, in fact, falls into three major units. There is an excellent and concise account of the early roots and formation of the Conference, with a summary of its first five decades—1904, the date of publication, was just two years following the Semi-Centennial Conference of 1902, held at Waverly, New York. The second division represents a biographical treatment, with photographs, of the preachers of the Conference, both living and dead. Each piece, as in the case of his own, cited above, gives appropriate biographical data, including educational background, information concerning conversion, an indication of special interests or involvements, publications, family, etc. Each ends with a record of Pastoral Appointments. This section represents a tradition now being cared for, in part, within the Memoirs section of our current Conference Journals. Chaffee was a real master, who crafted these sketches in a concise, factual, and non-sentimental manner, yet in a language that is reflective of late nineteenth-century values and style. The last section of this work contains a brief institutional history of each of the churches within the Conference, arranged by District, and including a record of those who served as Pastors. It would not be until 1963, when the Town and Country Commission of the Conference, under the supervision of the Rev. William A. Highfield, would publish, in mimeographed form, a post-Chaffee update of who, consecutively, served each of the appointments of the Conference.

In many ways, Chaffee's work remains the most useful Conference history published to date. In terms of its bulk, it is reminiscent of many county histories so popular in the last century, but Chaffee avoids a pre-packaged approach that made one county's story read like another. His is a work that is truly singular in the literature of Annual Conference histories.

LOUIS DEFOREST PALMER (1871-1968)

Of those who have made a substantial contribution to the historiography of our Conference, Louis DeForest Palmer is least known, and, unfortunately, infrequently recognized. In addition to being both the author and the publisher of the monograph, *Heroism and Romance: Early Methodism in Northeastern Pennsylvania*, Palmer distinguished himself by his service as a pastor, and by living to the rather extraordinary age of ninety-seven years. His book was published in 1950, and he died in 1968; yet, when Chaffee's work was published in 1904, Palmer had already been a member of the Conference for ten years! He was born on 13 January 1871, at Brookfield, New York; educated at the Norwich (New York) High School, and graduated with the degree A. B. from Syracuse University, 1901; in 1894, he united with the Wyoming Conference.[1]

Whereas Chaffee indicates that Palmer was married on 29 June 1899, to Miss Sadie Pauline Lewis, of Kattelville, New York,[2] J. Harold Davies, author of Palmer's memorial tribute, states that the wedding was on 28 June 1899, and that the bride's name was Sara Pollard Lewis.[3] "Sadie" might have been a diminutive, or affectionate rendering of "Sara," but the discrepancy between the reported middle names, and the date of the wedding, is a mystery.

Prior to his formal retirement in 1939, Palmer served the following churches:

> 1894 Coventry, 95-96 Gilbertsville, 97 Chenango Forks, 98-99 North Norwich, 00-02 Chenango Bridge, 03-06 Factoryville, 07-10 Owego, 11-15 Peckville, 16-17 Dunmore, 18-22 Ashley, 23-27 Norwich, 28-38 Clark's Summit, 39 Retired.[4]

In addition, Davies notes that for seventeen years after retirement, Palmer continued to serve as a pastor.[5] Unfortunately, pastoral records, as noted in the journals of that period, do not indicate service rendered beyond the year of retirement.

As the record shows, Palmer was recognized for his ability and contribution to the Conference. Davies also reports a Conference-level involvement which indirectly links Palmer with Chaffee, that of Conference boundaries:

> Wyoming Conference benefited greatly by his generously shared skills and abilities. Throughout his effective years he served on numerous Conference boards and agencies. Especially meaningful to him was his work on the Inter-Conference Commission on Conference Boundaries where he saw the need for redistributing the Conference. This took ten years of devoted effort and resulted in much creative change, though minimal within his own Conference.

A perusal of the journals of the fifties and early sixties reveals that the Palmers resided, from time to time, in Florida, New Mexico, and at State College, Pennsylvania, where, on 7 April 1968, he died, being survived by his wife of some sixty-eight years.[7]

Heroism and Romance is the product of many years of research, consultation with established scholars, and an imaginative and literary mind. Palmer is particularly careful with his use of primary materials, in most cases, personal journals, as well as secondary sources. He sought advice from historians at both Syracuse and at the State College at East Stroudsburg, Pennsylvania. He is sensitive to both the larger social and political issues of the period, and the personal, almost private, hopes and aspirations of those persons whose story he tells. This is reflected, in part, by the opening paragraph of his "Foreword":

> In these parlous days it is well for us to contemplate the toils, sacrifices and triumphs of men and women of another period in order that we may derive the incentives so needful for this present age. What were the conditions that hedged them about, what their limitations and what their achievements? Time's thievery is at greatest fault when it robs us of an awareness of the forgotten men and women of yesterday whose valorous living has made us their debtors for evermore.[8]

It can only be a matter of speculation as to why this work has not enjoyed wider circulation and comment. Perhaps it was seen as the work of an old man, no longer known by many of his colleagues; or, in light of the fact that a Conference-supported volume commemorating Wyoming's Centennial was already in process, perhaps it did not receive the type of endorsement it deserved. Regardless of the reasons, now unknown or forgotten, those of us who have read this work are indebted to its author.

The scope of the volume is defined both geographically and chronologically. In Palmer's words concerning place,

> Northeastern Pennsylvania, as here treated, comprehends that part of the Commonwealth that lies within the fan-shaped area beginning at the lower end of the Wyoming Valley and spreading out northeasterly to the Delaware river, as well as north and northwesterly to the state line. Taking the counties as they are now constituted, it embraces all of Susquehanna, Wayne and Lackawanna; all of Pike excepting the part that slopes southeasterly to the Delaware; all of Wyoming, excepting the southwestern corner; that part of Bradford along the Susquehanna and eastward; and such townships in Luzerne as include Plymouth, Jackson, Lehman and Lake on the west and Newport, Hanover, Fairview, Bear Creek and Buck on the south.[9]

The limitations of time are not so precisely defined. The *terminus ad quem* is the organization of the Oneida Conference on 10 June 1829, at Cazenovia, New York, when part of what we now know as the Wyoming Conference was taken from the Genessee Conference.[10] The *terminus ad quo* is more difficult to discover. In his introductory chapter, entitled, "The Background," Palmer writes of those Native Americans who lived within, or transported themselves through, the area. He describes the prolonged conflict known as the Yankee-

Pennamite War, ca. 1768-1784, as well as the region's involvement in the American Revolution.[11] Yet, there is, in this material, an event which informs and serves as a background for much of what follows. In a very real way, the Wyoming Massacre of 3-4 July 1778 marks the beginning of this history. I believe that for the closing decades of the eighteenth century, and for much of the nineteenth century, as well, the Wyoming Massacre served as a significant benchmark in the minds and imaginations of the people, in much the same way as the Agnes Flood of 1972 serves the Valley's inhabitants today.

In some ways, the work can also be seen as a partial biography of, and a testimony to, four men, whose presence and leadership were essential for the flowering and development of Methodism in Northeastern Pennsylvania: Anning Owen, a survivor of the Wyoming Massacre; William Colbert; Valentine Cook; and Thomas Ware. It is their story, the story of laymen become itinerant preachers, and in so doing, advancing Methodism throughout the region, that Palmer is able, and anxious, to tell.

The story of Dr. George Peck's early ministry in the area, beginning in the year 1818, is also told. Palmer is clearly an admirer of Peck's and makes significant use of his historical works as source material for his volume. The passages of Bishop Francis Asbury through the Valley and surrounding areas are noted by Palmer, who also supplies a rather concise, reflective, and straightforward assessment of Asbury's life and spirit and their influence on American Methodism:

> A matter of unusual note not only for Northeastern Pennsylvania but also for the whole church was the death of Bishop Francis Asbury, which took place on Sunday, March 31, 1816, in the seventy-first year of his age. For nearly forty-five years he had been an incessant preacher in America, nearly thirty-two of those years being a bishop. Naturally frail of body and beset by many maladies from which he suffered great pain for much of his life, he was a monumental example of devotion and of a will to serve in spite of all physical adversities and hindrances. In his labors he was the counterpart in America of John Wesley in the British Isles. Adhering closely to Wesley's system yet more understanding than Wesley as to the conditions in America, he made that system essentially American in its adaptation. Never affecting the role of a finished theologian or of a pulpit orator, he nevertheless excelled as a thinker and as a preacher of incisive utterance and of such knowledge of the Scriptures as to enable him to carry conviction with his hearers. As an administrator of the affairs of the church, whether at sessions of conferences or in the strategy of deploying the forces of the church, he was efficient and statesman-like. Given the unique opportunity of being present at and having large responsibility for the organic inception of Methodism in America, and afterward being commissioned with major supervision of the church, it was inevitable that very much of his personality entered permanently into its spirit and structure. His early and fairly frequent journeys along the Susquehanna river in the days of the pioneers gave inspiration and direction to the work in all of the Wyoming country, thus helping to establish Methodism in this region for all time to come. Even before the death of this great man the church here was well on its way to vaster things. Anning Owen, William Colbert, Valentine Cook, Thomas Ware and others had labored valiantly. However, their service was made much more valuable and meaningful because of the master mind and spirit of Francis Asbury.[12]

"Valuable" and "meaningful" are words which may also apply to the documentation of Methodism in the northeast corner of the Commonwealth of Pennsylvania, ca. 1778-1829, as written by Louis DeForest Palmer.

LEROY E. BUGBEE (1901-1974)

To his colleagues, he was known as Roy; to his students, as "Prof"; and to the Wyoming Conference, and the secondary school which shares its name, Leroy E. Bugbee was our centennial historian. Bugbee was born on 19 November 1901, in Boston, Massachusetts. In 1920 he graduated from Boston's Hyde Park High School and elected to continue his education at Boston University, from which he received his bachelor's degree in 1924, and his master's in 1925.

In September of 1925, he began his long relationship with Wyoming Seminary, where he served as a member of the faculty for forty-seven years, retiring in June of 1972. During this period, he did continuing education work at both Duke and Columbia Universities and traveled extensively in both the United States and Canada. At the time of his retirement, he was the Chairman of the Social Science and History Department.

In addition to his unique record of service to the school, Bugbee was viewed as a confidant and advisor to its chief administrators, was held in high esteem and affection by his colleagues and students, played a significant role in forming the academic style and direction of the school, and was chosen to author the school's history, *Wyoming Seminary: 1844-1944*. In preparation for the centennial celebration of the Wyoming Conference in 1952, Bugbee was asked to perform a similar function; he wrote *He Holds the Stars In His Hands*. In addition to these publications, he was active in, and wrote for, the Wyoming Historical and Geological Society of Wilkes-Barre.

In 1959, Bugbee was honored by the Freedoms Foundation of Valley Forge for his work on behalf of teaching responsible citizenship, by their Classroom Teacher's Medal Award. Two years following his retirement, in September of 1974, Leroy E. Bugbee died, leaving, in part, a legacy of many lives touched, and two useful, well written, institutional histories.[1]

Bugbee was, in many ways, a modest, if not a self-effacing, man. In the Preface to *Wyoming Seminary,* the author indicates that he has used a selection process, based on years of service to the school, in order to determine whose biography to include.[2] Although he meets these criteria himself, he omits himself, thus denying the reader of any autobiographical insight.

There is one anecdote which the author did include in the book, but the story is really about Levi Sprague:

> A number of years later after Sprague Hall was built the following incident occurred one Saturday afternoon to the writer. With that attention to minute details of administration which never interfered with his grasp of the larger principles and policies Dr. Sprague knocked at the door. Someone had told him the water in the dormitories had a bad taste and smell and he wanted to try it from a water faucet in a teacher's apartment. He came through the bedroom to the bath and turned the water on tasting it and smelling it. What he thought of the water the writer has no recollection but as he turned to go out his eye caught sight of the single bed of the bachelor's quarters. He hesitated a moment and then with a twinkle in his eye he said, "You should have twin beds, Professor." After a comment or two about modern living and twin beds, he added, "We like to have our faculty members marry, settle down, and stay a life time at the Seminary."[3]

In a brief passage, concerning the creation and development of the History Department—the very department which Bugbee would chair for many years—he refers to himself only twice, and then, as "the writer."[4]

At Seminary, Bugbee was viewed by many of his students as one member of a special faculty group, sometimes referred to as the "Four Horsemen." In addition to Bugbee, it included Edwin J. Roberts, Theodore S. Abbot, and Horace S. Parker. All were from New England and seemed to share a similar Yankee value structure. Bugbee's affection for these men is apparent to the reader of their biographical sketches.[5]

To the student of Conference history, the value of *Wyoming Seminary* lies in the fact that the book not only documents, carefully and comprehensively, the history of the school, but it also demonstrates just how closely the school was tied to the Conference. It was, for many years, a symbiotic relationship, where patterns of leadership, financing, recruitment, philosophy, and institutional health were almost inseparable. It is difficult for the contemporary reader, who knows something of the present relationship of the two institutions—meaningful, yet carefully defined and circumspect—to appreciate fully just how closely linked the school was to the Conference, and the Conference to the school. Even after one hundred years, in 1944, Bugbee is both sensitive to and appreciative of this fact. He dedicates this volume to Dr. George Peck, who first preached on the need for such a school; to the Rev. William Reddy, the school's first benefactor and fund-raiser; and to the school's first Board of Trustees, elected by the Oneida Conference, who had the vision and foresight to choose Reuben Nelson as its first Principal.[6] Particularly with reference to the nineteenth century, *Wyoming Seminary* is a critical source for those interested in the Conference's history.

The book also addresses, albeit indirectly, one of the more significant transitions which occurred within the hearts and minds of religious people, specifically Methodists, in this nation. I write of the acceptance of the need for sound education. By sharing with the reader the story of the school's early struggle for survival, Bugbee is not only writing of institutional viability; he is also commenting upon the Conference's growing acceptance and affirmation of the school. We need to remember that in the early part of the last century, Conferences were made up of preachers only, and that the need for an educated clergy, as opposed to the unlettered lay preacher, had by no means been established.[7]

Bugbee begins his Conference centennial history, *He Holds The Stars In His Hands,* by re-telling a Chaffee story, reminiscent of Benjamin Franklin's ruminations about a rising or a setting sum:

> It was warm and sunny in the city of Carbondale. Many visitors had spent the night with families of the community and more visitors were driving into town with the coolness of early morning. Shortly before nine o'clock of the beginning of Wednesday, July 7, 1852, the large "extraordinarily sweet-toned bell" in the Methodist Church steeple rang so that all the townspeople might know this was the hour for the first session of the Wyoming Annual Conference of the Methodist Episcopal Church. It was a cheerful, melodious note summoning the people on foot and in carriages to the church. Just before nine o'clock the ringing ceased and then after several minutes the same bell sounded the hour of the town clock with the same melodious note. Most of the members of the new

Conference had assembled in the church by the time the last stroke of the bell had sounded from the tower.

It was a beautiful white building ". . . decidedly the best and most expensive Protestant church in the city . . ." The style of architecture was the New England colonial with the classic facade, two Doric columns framing the doorway. The belfry rose from a square fenced platform leading the upward by its symmetry and beauty. "Upon the top of the belfry was a weather vane, called by some 'an eagle,' by others 'a dove,' and by others 'a goose.' " What the symbol was, the coming century would determine.[8]

In many ways, the book attempts to answer the question in ways that leave open the possibility for both ongoing and future assessment.

In addition to dealing with many individuals and groups which have played a significant role in the development of the Conference, Bugbee, as in his work *Wyoming Seminary,* deals with some of the significant social and intellectual movements and transitions experienced by both the Conference and the national church. Chapters 3 and 4 document the metamorphosis from camp meeting to outdoor Christian Education; Chapter 5 deals with many attempts to establish a Conference school; Chapter 7 speaks of the social ministry performed by Deaconesses and the establishment of the Children's Home; and in Chapter 9, there is some indication of how the church responded to the great waves of immigration. These are significant movements, for they reveal something of our denomination's growing self-awareness, and its developing commitment to multi-faceted ministry and mission.

The weaknesses inherent in any institutional history are, first, that it will be transparently self-serving, and second, that as its reporting becomes increasingly contemporary, it will also grow proportionately less reliable. For the most part, Bugbee has been able to avoid these traps. His are friendly and celebratory histories; yet they are not beyond an occasional critical allusion or insight. They are upbeat, positive, and even inspirational, yet not disporportionately so. And, like any good history, they encourage the reader to explore as yet unanswered questions.

Something of the triumphalistic mood of the nineteen-fifties is reflected in Bugbee's conclusion to *He Holds The Stars In His Hands,* but that is not all there is. There is also a strong and abiding sense of appreciation for the many ways in which the Spirit touched individual and corporate lives for the good:

Times have changed, yet the spiritual needs of the membership and the abiding truths the preachers seek to reveal are the same. Everything is different; yet nothing has changed—Straight is the way and narrow the gate that leads to eternal life, and few there be who shall find it. This can never change. The wilderness and the circuit rider have vanished, but the way of life they preached remains. The loud Amen Corner and the hallelujahs have gone, but the faith, the willingness to serve and sacrifice remain. Over the Conference session of 1952 the long shadows of great men will fall: Dr. George Peck with his eloquence, his great faith and powerful leadership; William Wyatt with his wit, his great sincerity and his aggressive gospel; Reuben Nelson with his capacity to mold the young, to organize and manage the affairs of the Church and to train new leaders like Dr. Levi L. Sprague. But of equal significance will be the gallery filled with the devout and the faithful—the preachers and the laymen who with their wives served their generation that God might live in the hearts of men forever. Austin Griffin, preacher, Presiding Elder and member of the Wyoming Conference for 56 years, spoke these words in 1905 which

with beautiful symbol ring as true today and for tomorrow as they did yesterday: "Christ
still walks among the 'golden candlesticks' and He holds the stars in His hands.'"[9]

We also rejoice that the Spirit touched the life of this small-bodied, unpretentious man, who carefully and skillfully crafted these fine histories.

A great deal has been accomplished by our Conference historians in the area of discovering and revealing what, to the untrained eye, would remain as "things unseen." Movement and development are made real by their insistent commitment to biographical sketch and personal anecdote. Institutional history is liberated from its bondage to facts and figures by their ability to see, and, in part, communicate, what was, in fact, a venture in faith. Their broader vision and understanding enables the reader to link the local setting and area administration of the church to both the larger national connection, of which we are a part, and the Body of Christ, into which we are grafted. And, perhaps most significantly of all, these histories, written by George Peck, Amasa Franklin Chaffee, Louis D. Palmer, and Leroy E. Bugbee, as well written and comprehensive as they are, never take upon themselves the assumption of being exhaustive. They reveal only part of what was unseen or unknown, in a style which encourages the contemporary student and scholar to explore new or unanswered questions.

With deep thanksgiving, we express our gratitude to those who have gone before, and look, with much hope, to those who will surely follow.

END NOTES

Introduction

[1]Fred D. Gealy, Austin C. Lovelace, Carlton R. Young, Emory Stevens Bucke (editors), *Companion to the Hymnal: A Handbook to the 1964 Methodist Hymnal* (Nashville: Abingdon Press, 1970), p. 296.

GEORGE PECK (1797-1876)

1. Matthew Simpson, *Cyclopaedia of Methodism* (Philadelphia: Louis H. Everts, 1880), p. 698.

2. A. F. Chaffee, *History of the Wyoming Conference of the Methodist Episcopal Church* (New York: Eaton and Mains, 1904), pp. 222-223.

3. George Peck, *Wyoming: Its History, Stirring Incidents, and Romantic Adventures* (New York: Harper and Brothers, 1860), p. 234. The citation is from an article on Frances Slocum.

4. George Peck, *Early Methodism Within the Bounds of the Old Genessee Conference from 1788 to 1828.* (New York: Carlton and Porter, 1860). The citation is from the Preface, no pagination given.

5. George Peck, *The Life and Times of George Peck, D. D.* (New York: Nelson and Phillips, 1874), p. 249.

6. Arthur E. Jones, Jr., "The Years of Disagreement, 1844-61," Chapter 16, in Volume II, *The History of American Methodism,* Emory Stevens Bucke, General Editor (Nashville: Abingdon Press, 1964), pp. 144-205.

7. George Peck, *The Life and Times of George Peck, D. D.,* p. 409.

AMASA FRANKLIN CHAFFEE (1855-1926)

1. A. F. Chaffee, *History of the Wyoming Conference of the Methodist Episcopal Church* (New York: Eaton and Mains, 1904), pp. 297-298.

2. *Journal* of the Wyoming Annual Conference, 1905, p. 12.

3. Leroy E. Bugbee, *He Holds the Stars in His Hands* (The Wyoming Annual Conference of the Methodist Church, 1952), pp. 249-251.

4. *Journal* of the Colorado Annual Conference, 1908.

5. *Journal* of the Kansas Annual Conference, 1927, pp. 333-334. I am indebted to Dr. Kenneth Rowe, Methodist Librarian at the History and Archives Center, Drew University, for his research and assistance concerning Chaffee's Pastoral Record following his transfer in 1905.

6. Leroy E. Bugbee, *He Holds the Stars in His Hands,* p. 249.

LOUIS DEFOREST PALMER (1871-1968)

1. A. F. Chaffee, *History of the Wyoming Conference, op. cit.,* p. 380.

2. *Ibid.*

3. *Journal* of the Wyoming Annual Conference, 1968, p. 252.

4. *Journal* of the Wyoming Annual Conference, 1967, p. 258.

5. *Journal* of the Wyoming Annual Conference, 1968, p. 252.

6. *Ibid.*

7. *Ibid.*

8. Louis DeForest Palmer, *Heroism and Romance: Early Methodism in Northeastern Pennsylvania* (Saylorsburg, Pennsylvania: Engel-Truitt Press, private publication by the Author, 1950). The citation is from the "Foreword," no pagination given.

9. Louis DeForest Palmer, *Heroism and Romance,* pp. 1-2.

10. *Ibid.* p. 231.

11. *Ibid.* pp. 1-34, *passim.*

12. *Ibid.* pp. 194-195.

LEROY E. BUGBEE (1901-1974)

1. I am indebted to Dr. Wallace F. Stettler, President of Wyoming Seminary, who first supplied me with this biographical material.

2. Leroy E. Bugbee, *Wyoming Seminary: 1844-1944* (Private publication). The citation is from the "Preface," pp. ix-x.

3. *Ibid.,* p. 437.

4. *Ibid.,* pp. 702-703.

5. *Ibid.,* p. 804 ff.

6. *Ibid.,* "Dedication," no pagination given.

7. Gerald O. McCulloh, *Ministerial Education in the American Methodist Movement* (Nashville: United Methodist Board of Higher Education and Ministry, 1980), p. 19 ff.

8. Leroy E. Bugbee, *He Holds the Stars in His Hands* (Scranton, Pennsylvania: The Wyoming Annual Conference of the Methodist Church, 1952), p. 1

9. *Ibid.,* pp. 279-280.

REVIVAL BEGINNINGS

Charles H. Lippy

> On Monday the crowd had retired, but there was still a large number
> of earnest listeners to the services on the ground. In the morning, after an
> appropriate discourse, the sacrament of the Lord's Supper was ad-
> ministered. It was a melting occasion. After the service the mourners were
> invited into the altar, and although it would contain a hundred persons it
> was soon filled, and numbers hung upon the railing weeping. The poles
> were removed, and when those who desired prayers, and those who came
> forward to labor with them, were upon their knees, a large space extending
> from the stand out among the seats prepared for the congregation was
> densely filled. Now a murmur was heard coming up from the mass of
> earnest oppressed spirits. One led in prayer until his voice was drowned
> with the wailings of the seekers and groan and intercessions of the pious
> who were mingling among them, and fully entering into their sympathies.
> A scene of holy confusion now followed. It was a deep-toned roar like the
> voice of many waters. One incessant tide of prayer and praise rolled on for
> many hours. No pause was called for, either for refreshment or for
> preaching. One and another, and sometimes half a dozen together, would
> break their chains and shout "Glory to God!" and then commence labor-
> ing for others. The prayer-meeting was only interrupted at twelve o'clock
> for *a midnight cry,* and was then resumed and continued until sunrise.

—George Peck

Revivalism, wrote historian William McLoughlin, "is the Protestant
ritual . . . in which charismatic evangelists convey 'the Word' of God to large
masses of people who, under this influence, experience what Protestants call
conversion, salvation, regeneration, or spiritual rebirth."[1] He went on to
argue that:

> Great awakenings (and the revivals that are part of them) are the results, not of
> depressions, wars, or epidemics, but of critical disjunctions in our self-understanding.
> They are not brief out-bursts of mass emotionalism by one group or another but profound
> cultural transformations affecting all Americans and extending over a generation or
> more.[2]

McLoughlin's comments provide at least a focus for considering the
emergence of Methodism in what is now the Wyoming Conference of the
United Methodist Church. First, revivals are a form of religious ritual. That
is, revivals consist of identifiable components which repeatedly recur in much
the same fashion. Ritual is central to human life, offering a steady rhythm by
which persons mark those extraordinary events and occasions which encap-
sule life's deepest meaning. For example, the ritual of the Lord's Supper
denotes the way Christians re-create the formative act of their faith, but it
also invites believers to recall and renew their commitment to those symbols

of sacrificial love on which the Christian life bases meaning and binds Christians past and present into a single community. So, too, with the ritual of revivals. Revivals supply one form by which individuals proclaim their identity with the Christian family through an experience of conversion dramatically enacted according to a standardized process.

McLoughlin's remarks also remind us that revivals are directly related to one style of religious experience, one which generates radical change in the orientation of human life. At least since the time of William James nearly a century ago, students of religion have seen conversion as that religious experience in which one exchanges a particular set of values or a particular way of searching for meaning in life for another.[3] This new source of meaning confronts the convert as coming directly from God and demands a response. One must either abandon one's past direction and accept a more authentic source of meaning, or reject ultimate truth and lose hope for fulfillment in this life or the next. But conversion does not strike in a vacuum. Generally the convert has been groping for a sense of purpose in life, a way to endow the maze of day-to-day experiences with meaning.

Following McLoughlin, much of this unsettledness stems from external forces—what McLoughlin termed "cultural transformations." Rapid, seemingly uncontrollable social change may well be the most important of these transformations which foster the revival ethos. In our own day, there is ample evidence of this kind of social transition: the threat of nuclear holocaust appears beyond our control, the economic turmoil occasioned by inflation and recession makes us feel powerless, and a highly complex industrialized urban civilization seems to destroy the stability provided by the traditional family structure. Other forces were at work in American society in the nineteenth century when Wyoming Conference Methodism* gained strength through revivals, forces as critical as a sense of personal sin in making revival conversions peculiarly fitting for thousands.

Three waves of revivalism gave impetus to Wyoming Conference Methodism. At the beginning of the nineteenth century, camp meetings emerged as vehicles for communicating the means to find a new sense of values and direction in life. In time, the camp meeting became so potent a mechanism for conveying religious truth that it became institutionalized, permanent grounds were acquired, and regular times for meetings scheduled. But in its early years, the camp meeting found its most congenial home on the frontier, though it is hard today to envision the area encompassed by the Wyoming Conference as a frontier, an untamed wilderness which could enrich or engulf human existence, depending on how humans approached it. As towns grew and population increased so that churches

---

*I have attempted to restrict reference to particular churches to ones which are presently part of the Wyoming Conference. In addition, I frequently refer to the present Wyoming Conference as denoting a geographical region as well as an annual conference. Much of the Wyoming Conference territory, prior to the organization of the annual conference in 1858, was part of the old Genessee Conference. For purposes of clarity and familiarity, however, I have not made mention of the Genessee Conference in the text.

could be established and maintained, the massive revivals of the 1830s and 1840s saw hundreds in the Wyoming, Chenango, and Susquehanna Valleys make their way to Methodist altars and find the key to what life was really about. But growing pains came to nations as to individuals. By mid-century, when the nation spanned the continent, divisions over slavery and the revival of millions of new immigrants threatened to destroy the ideals which had given birth to the United States. Another wave of revivalism, known as the "holiness movement," swept the land, issuing a mighty call to religious experience as the means to transform social and personal chaos into order.

In the pages which follow, I shall show how and why each of these waves of revivalism was essential to the cultivation of Methodism in the Wyoming Conference. Then I shall examine the ways in which revivalism continues to shape not only Methodism in this region, but also American religious life as a whole. Finally, I shall indicate why the revival heritage and the Methodist vision of the Christian proclamation have enjoyed a companionship which now stretches over nearly two centuries.

I

The date and place of the first camp meeting in the United States are lost to history. But in Logan County, Kentucky, in 1800, and at Cane Ridge, Kentucky, in 1801, revival camp meetings gained such wide-spread attention that the camp meeting became a fixture of frontier life.[4] Often the camp meetings arose seemingly spontaneously, but in Methodist circles frequently in connection with quarterly meetings. Methodist circuit rider Henry Smith, for example, noted that:

> people went out far and near to sacramental and quarterly meetings, with no intention of staying on the ground, but intended either to return home or lodge somewhere in the neighborhood where the camp meeting was held; but so many were smitten to the ground, and continued in a helpless state, apparently insensible to everything around them and so continued for hours, some for twenty-four hours, that their friends had to stay and take care of them. . . . Many said "The next time I go to one of these meetings, I'll go prepared to stay on the ground." Others who were obliged to leave the meetings, soon returned with wagon or carts etc, to stay on the ground during their continuance, for many hundreds were obliged to go away.[5]

Methodist pioneer Peter Cartwright, in his autobiography, provided a classic description of what transpired at the camp meeting:

> [People] would erect their camps with logs or frame them, and cover them with clapboards or shingles. They would also erect a shed, sufficiently large to protect five thousand people from wind and rain, and cover it with boards or shingles; build a large stand, seat the shed, and here they would collect together from forty to fifty miles around, sometimes further than that. Ten, twenty, and sometimes thirty ministers, of different denominations would come together and preach night and day, four or five days together; and, indeed, I have known these camp-meetings to last three or four weeks, and a great good resulted from them. I have seen more than a hundred sinners fall like dead men under one powerful sermon, and I have seen and heard more than five hundred Christians all shouting aloud the high praises of God at these camp-meetings.[6]

Time and again the pattern was repeated: a speakers' platform; seating, usually separated by gender, for lay persons; an altar area where those anxious for their souls would gather near the speaker to await confrontation with the Divine.[7] And soon the camp meeting assumed the character of a ritual form: the assembling of people at the site, an opening service filled with singing, time for family prayers each morning before a community prayer service, a morning service often featuring testimony from recent converts, a preaching service, afternoon and evening services, time for clergy to counsel privately with individuals, and, frequently, a closing Love Feast and a departing service when the camp was broken up. But the conversion experience itself also assumed a ritual form.[8] First came awareness of the evils of one's past life and a time of conviction, often lasting several hours or even several days, that one must separate from the life of the world. At this point, transition to a new religious identity was underway, for a person under conviction is neither the sinner of the past nor the convert of the future, but in a state of flux. During this time of ambiguity, many felt the power of God at work, sometimes striking outbrusts of shouting or convulsive movements, until one had assurance that a new order had come to life, that one had a new identity which would allow one to control the untamed forces which haunted life in the wilderness.

The phenomenon of the camp meeting spread to all areas of the frontier, including Pennsylvania and New York. Much of the land which now comprises the Wyoming Conference was frontier when Methodist pioneer Anning Owen and the first circuit riders roamed across its hills and valleys. It was not open to settlement until the close of the War for Independence, for British colonial policy had discouraged or prohibited westward movement, in order to maintain a buffer zone between communities along the Atlantic seaboard, and the land west of the Appalachian mountain chain reserved for the Native American Indian tribes.

The gradual migration of the population westward brought not only the contagious excitement of constructing a society from raw materials (human and otherwise), but also an incalculable degree of social dislocation.[9] Ties were severed with family and friends who may have lived in the same small geographic area (most likely in New England), bringing the loss of tribal or community identity and the sense of a personal past. Gone, too, were the amenities of civilization, such as they were: fledgling educational institutions, embryonic political structures, developing medical assistance, and the like. Persons on the frontier, whether in Kentucky or New York, were a people without roots, striving to carve civilization out of the wilderness. Thrust into an ethos where the struggle to survive was more fact than fiction, the call to conversion trumpeted by evangelists whose gaze was fixed on things eternal struck many as a viable alternative to the vagaries of empirical reality. The human associations nurtured among those who came to the camp meetings were a welcome relief from the solitariness of life in a land sparsely populated. For the women, especially, the camp meeting provided an avenue for self-expression. It was not uncommon for women to shatter the sexist taboos of the day by bursting into public prayer or crying out for salvation. And the religious message itself was potent. While camp meeting sermons may have stretched two hours or more, their appeal was direct and their content simple. The appeal was to the heart, to the "religious affections" as eighteenth-century Puritan divine Jonathan Edwards had called the forces aroused in revivals. If one experienced the work of God within, one could be certain one's life was secure under God's providence, no matter how uncertain day-to-day life remained.

The camp meeting fervor swept across the Wyoming Conference. George Peck and A. F. Chaffee, chroniclers of Methodism's history in this area, enumerated some twenty-six camp meetings and sixteen revivals in Wyoming Conference in the first three decades of the nineteenth century.[10] Camp meetings, for example, were held in or near Forty Fort, Kingston, Honesdale, and Hop Bottom, while revivals came to Kirkwood, Cooperstown, Owego, and Candor, to mention just a few. While they may not have attracted the numbers which Cartwright claimed for the camp meetings and revivals of the old Southwest, many began in the humble barns of ordinary folk at Methodist quarterly meetings. Like the camp meetings in the old Southwest, those in the Wyoming Conference assumed a definite pattern, and the conversion experience became a definable process. Witness George Peck's account of a conversion in connection with a camp meeting held near Forty Fort in 1817:

> A company of young people from Forty Fort had a tent on the ground, and, for persons who made no pretensions to religion, were unusually interested in the exercises. At the close of the meeting it was evident that the Spirit of God was at work in their hearts. Not being sufficiently humbled to come out and seek religion openly, and yet feeling so deeply awakened as to resolve upon a change of life in some form, the leading spirit in the group [Betsey Myers] fixed her plan to escape from the camp-ground early on the morning of the close without exposing herself to the multitude, and to seek religion at home. The Myers tent was early taken down, and everything was in readiness to lead the procession of wagons and carriages down the mountain into the settlement. Betsey was so deeply wounded that she lost her power of self-control and wept bitterly. In passing through the deep ravine called Carpenter's Notch [the site of camp meetings in 1819 and 1820] she sobbed and cried aloud. As the carriage moved out of the dense shade and entered the outskirts of the valley settlement, her cries became so loud that they were heard by those who were next in the train. The carriage paused, and on the invitation of a female friend, a daughter of Colonel Denison, Betsey Myers alighted from the wagon and fell upon her knees in the shade of a clump of oak and pine shrubs by the side of the road, crying "God have mercy upon me a poor wicked sinner!" The way was soon blocked up. The whole train was arrested and the attention of all was attracted to a little group of young ladies by the wayside weeping and praying. The preachers came along and they found agreeable work upon their hands there on their way from the encampment. Other penitents joined the group, and there the voice of prayer, earnest prayer, ascended to heaven. It was not long before shouts of victory and songs of praise varied the exercises, and now here was the rare scene of a miniature camp-meeting by the wayside.
>
> The attention of the neighborhood was attracted, and people came to the spot to see what was the matter who there sought and found salvation. For several hours the scenes of the camp-meeting altar were witnessed in that apparently chance collection of people on the highway. Cries of penitents were succeeded by shouts of deliverance until some ten or a dozen were happily converted to God.[11]

In an unpublished essay, written in pencil in 1870 when he was living in Scranton, Peck reflected on why the camp meetings spawned such cataclysmic conversions.[12] The continuous services, spanning several days or weeks, made a deeper impression on people than regular weekly or intermittent circuit services, he claimed. Peck also pointed to the novelty of the camp meeting structure, its creation of a special setting and series of events, as a means for attracting those hitherto unidentified with Christianity to religious activities. Likewise, the format of the camp meeting provided a break from the tedious routine of wilderness life which was "favorable to the emotions." Finally, camp meeting preaching, aimed at the conscience and not a "display of fine points" of theology, was more conducive to eliciting conversions than ordinary sermons.

But individual conversions were far from the only result of the camp meetings. Indeed, some seventy-five churches in the Wyoming Conference trace their origins to classes and preaching stations established first in the heyday of the frontier revival. Congregations at Barton, Fly Creek, Greene, Norwich, Carbondale, Bainbridge, Trucksville, and Newark Valley are among those with roots in this period. But the establishment of classes, preaching stations, and churches was itself a sign of cultural transformation. It meant that population was growing and becoming sufficiently concentrated that social institutions could be supported and maintained. It meant the end of the wilderness.

II

By the mid-1820s, the frontier that had been the Wyoming Conference was rapidly disappearing. In New York, for example, the opening of the Erie Canal in 1825 altered the social landscape dramatically. The prospect of jobs lured many to seek their fortunes along the route of the Canal and in nearby territory. The expansion of markets for manufactured goods brought the rise of the factory village, signalling the urbanization and industrialization that was to transform the American character within two generations. The phenomenal prosperity that followed such rapid expansion brought new immigrants to the country, persons increasingly of an alien cultural and religious background, whose presence seemed to threaten the religious and political values folk saw as hallmarks of the American way. President Andrew Jackson came to symbolize the dawning age. Of humble frontier origins, Jackson espoused the ideals of democracy and progress through the industry of the "common man."[13] Jackson was also the first president to ride on the railroad, that newfangled means of transportation which was to link at least the northern and western parts of the nation and in its own way attempt to forge a homogeneous civilization out of the American people. Many looked at American society and felt that the resources were at hand to erect the Kingdom of God on earth. Some banded in "voluntary societies" to reform those areas of common life not yet under the rule of God, attacking everything, from intemperance to slavery, which marred their utopian vision. But the enthusiasm of visionaries met stumbling blocks. The age of Jackson saw the beginnings of the forced removal of native American tribes to western reservations. Economic growth came to a grinding halt with the depression of 1837. And despite the ever more strident calls of reformers, slavery did not disappear, but became a cancer eating at the heart of the nation. It was the country's adolescence. Again, social transformations were wreaking havoc with personal and collective identity.

Some sought to bring order to their lives by embracing new religious alternatives. Hundreds followed John Humphrey Noyes in a radical experiment in communal living near Oneida, New York, based on the conviction that only through withdrawal from the broader social order could one attain perfect spirituality. Out of central New York also came Joseph Smith, with his proclamation of the religious truth contained in the *Book of Mormon*. Yet others experimented with spiritualism and communication with the dead, while many expected the imminent return of the Christ to bring an end to the cultural malaise. Some blamed the social turmoil on the growing number of Roman Catholics invading an overwhelmingly Protestant culture. But in certain circles, there arose the conviction that a revival of religion in its old-fashioned form, the form the previous generation found in the enthusaism of the camp meeting, would transform the chaos of America's adolescence into the order of adulthood.[14]

The central figure of the evangelical revivalism of the 1830s and 1840s was Charles Grandison Finney, and the revival which catapulted him to fame occurred in 1830-31 in Rochester, New York, one of the new urban areas which owed its existence to the Erie Canal, westward movement, and a nascent industrialization.[15] Finney's genius lay in his ability to recast the ritual forms of the frontier camp meeting for an urbanized audience. The result became known as "new measures" revivalism. Convinced that revivals did not arise spontaneously through divine intervention, Finney developed strategies which, he believed, could generate a revival of true religion whenever properly implemented.[16] These techniques included holding services at "unseasonable hours" (times other than Sundays or evenings); having an "anxious bench," like the pen before the altar at camp meetings where those under conviction might sit; scheduling "protracted meetings," that is, holding a revival which spanned several weeks or months; setting up "inquiry meetings" and house-to-house visits for those uncertain of their spiritual status; using colloquial language, avoiding deep theology, offering emotionally charged prayers, and naming specific individuals thought unsaved in sermons; and organizing special "cottage meetings" or home prayer meetings for women. Finney was also convinced that individuals did not need some miraculous divine intrusion into their lives to bring conversion. Rather, he saw conversion as an act of the human will, a choice anyone could make at any time. In his mind, salvation was an invitation God issued moment by moment, not a process in which God chose a select few to convert.

Others quickly adopted "new measures" techniques, although some objected to the emotionalism of it all, as well as to the idea that revivals could be orchestrated by human manipulation of particular methods. In the 1830s and 1840s evangelists fanned the flames of so many revivals in upstate New York that the region became known as the "burned-over" district. And while Finney was not a Methodist, it was the Methodist movement that benefited most from the "new measures" awakening, just as it had reaped the greatest results from the frontier camp meetings.[17] Finney's insistence that conversion was the outcome of a human decision was particularly germane to the Methodist style, for the Wesleyan approach had long maintained that salvation was a co-operative endeavor: God in Christ effected the means of salvation, but each person had to decide individually whether to accept or reject divine grace.

By highlighting the role of the individual in salvation, "new measures" revivalism also meshed with the cultural transformations sweeping Jacksonian America.[18] It granted persons the power to control their own destinies in a world out of control. It made individuals important in an age when expansion, urbanization, industrialization, immigration, and sectional rivalries overwhelmed common folk and left them adrift in a society where the old ways no longer worked. It provided a release from the tensions and pressures of adjusting to rapid social change. And the adaptation of the style of the frontier camp meeting to an increasingly urban setting offered contact with the familiar, when the social order seemed more alien and strange.

The northern fringes of the Wyoming Conference were on the edge of the "burned-over" district, and within the present Wyoming Conference, many powerful revivals transpired during the period from 1830 to 1850, and many camp meetings were held to perpetuate the old religious message. Peck and Chaffee, identifying only those meetings and revivals of "especial power," noted over fifty major camp meeting gatherings and revivals in these two decades, including those at North Afton, Oneonta, Flemingville, and Factoryville. More than seventy new churches, classes, or preaching stations were established within the Wyoming Conference. Methodist work in Binghamton (Centenary), Vestal, Lake Como, Meshoppen, Beach Lake, Noxen, and Clarks Green—to note a few—stems from this era. Yet, the major wave of revivals to shape Wyoming Conference Methodism came in the 1850s and 1860s, when a passion for spiritual holiness consumed the souls and minds of millions of Americans.

III

For a generation of Christians converted in the early camp meetings, the revivals engineered by evangelicals such as Finney provided a confirmation of the authenticity of their own religious experience. Many who accepted the gift of salvation as they sat on anxious benches or knelt at altars had previously experienced the miracle of grace. Under the evangelist's spell, they sought reassurance that their destinies were secure. So it was also for the generation first awakened by the evangelical revivalists. As time went on, the ardor of conversion itself began to wane, and as American society continued to change, there was a need to know with absolute certainty that one's religious affirmation would continue to endow life with purpose.

A casual look at American society revealed that the expectations of the revivalists were yet unfulfilled. Record numbers of conversions and attempts to reform the social order had not transformed the United States into the Kingdom of God on earth. Immigration mushroomed, bringing over large numbers of people who did not share the evangelical perspective to America. As mid-century approached, nativist xenophobia grew at an unprecedented rate. Political demagogues, both North and South, fueled the regional hostility symbolized in opposition to or support for slavery. Wittingly or unwittingly, the nation had embarked on the course that would lead to the Civil War. Through most of the 1850s, though, the economy prospered. But in 1857 came a severe, though brief depression which augmented the general malaise as it shattered the evangelicals' hopes that America could become the Redeemer's nation. Emanating largely from the labors of New York Methodist laywoman Phoebe Palmer, this revival stressed the ideas of sanctification (holiness) and Christian perfection, both central to Methodist teaching. Phoebe Palmer, despite an earlier conversion, had become spiritually discontent. Conversion alone was simply not enough. As Mrs. Palmer read and prayed, she became convinced that conversion was but the first blessing offered the Christian. It set the believer on the right road, but did not bring one to the end of the religious quest. In Wesley's writings concerning holiness and perfection, she found the promise of a "second blessing" which would come to those who had grown in grace, an experience of sanctification in which the convert became a holy person. To a large extent, this "second blessing" was a confirming experience which reinforced the authenticity of conversion. But a dramatic experience of sanctification was also the religious expression of the idea of progress. If social progress had not yet recast the United States into the heavenly Kingdom, spiritual progress could mold the believer into a paragon of holiness. The barriers which thwarted realization of the social vision—sectionalism, slavery, non-Protestant immigrants, and the like—need not deter the individual's progress towards perfection.

Mrs. Palmer's quest for the "second blessing" initially took the form of organizing prayer groups for women, a form with roots in the cottage meetings of the evangelical revivals, as well as the benevolent societies, whose active membership was largely female. But the prayer meetings were also occasions of serious religious inquiry, as the devout analyzed their spiritual progress. Largely through her husband's business connections, and both Palmers' Methodist association, the quest for true holiness soon engulfed men as well as women, and businessmen began organizing lunch hour prayer groups and similar gatherings. The press publicized the movement, and by 1858, the passion for holiness had spread from New York to California. Some of the earlier "new measures" revivalists became swept away by the pursuit of perfection. Charles G. Finney, for example, devoted much of his later life to expounding on the idea of perfection. In his memoirs, he wrote:

> . . . one of our theological students arose, and put the inquiry, whether the Gospel did not provide for Christians, all the conditions of an established faith, and hope, and love; whether there was not something better and higher than Christians had generally experienced;
> in short, whether sanctification was not attainable in this life; that is, scantification in such a sense that Christians could have unbroken peace, and not come into condemnation, or have the feeling of condemnation or a consciousness of sin. Brother [Asa] Mahan immediately answered, "Yes." What occurred at this meeting, brought the question of

santification prominently before us, as a practical question. We had no theories on the subject, no philosophy to maintain, but simply took it up as a Bible question.[21]

The holiness revivals again stressed inner experience rather than creed or the fine points of theology. Realization that one had received the "second blessing" was a matter of the heart, not the head. Given Methodism's emphasis on inner experience as the locus of true religion, it is no wonder that Methodists responded to the search for holiness in massive numbers. The revivals also offered fresh assurance that those converted in the earlier evangelical surge had a secure faith, in a time when American society was reaching the breaking point. Of course, the holiness revivals also brought hundreds to the awareness that they had control over their own destinies, in the simple acceptance of the gift of salvation. Then, too, the revivals revitalized common life in an age of great transformation. Rich or poor, immigrant or native, abolitionist or advocate of slavery—all had a unity which transcended social categories in the experience of sanctification. When surface differences disappeared, a true union based on the heart might prevail. The holiness revivals also gained strength because their message of progress, of growth in grace, of striving for perfection, harmonized with the spirit of the age, which saw progress towards the perfect society as the intended *raison d'etre* of the American nation.

The holiness revivals left their mark on Wyoming Conference Methodism. In the early years of the holiness movement, the present Wyoming Conference was organized in Carbondale, Pennsylvania, in 1852. That same year a major revival came to Carbondale. Between 1850 and 1870, nearly eighty-five revivals brought the message of progress toward sanctification to those living within the Conference. In the peak years of 1857-58 alone, the revival fires were stoked at Kingston, East Lynn, East Bridgewater (near Montrose), Susquehanna, Gilbertsville, Hawley, Davenport, Milford, Schenevus, and Flemingville. And thirty-five new churches, classes, or preaching stations were established to minister to the spiritual hunger of a growing population. For example, Methodism in Dunmore, Hornbrook, Dalton, Sayre, and West Pittston traces its heritage to the holiness revivals, as do such churches as Binghamton's Tabernacle and High Street, Asbury and Court Street in Scranton, and Derr Memorial and Parrish Street, Wilkes-Barre.

IV

The frontier camp meeting now rests in history, the anxious benches of "new measures" revivalism have disappeared, and the achievement of holiness has again been relegated to the few, rather than expected of the masses. But the revival heritage lives on.

One of the first efforts to perpetuate the heritage came in the move to make the camp meeting a permanent feature of Methodist religious life. Once the wilderness had vanished, the move to establish permanent camp grounds logically resulted from the desire to pass on to succeeding generations the religious certainty found in the conversion experience.

Within the Wyoming Conference, the "permanent" camp grounds at Dimock and Sidney Grove are most well-known.[22] The current programs at Ocean Grove, New Jersey, continue the heritage, as evidenced by the name of their sponsoring society: the Ocean Grove Camp Meeting Association. In time, though, the camp meeting became anachronistic. The more urban and industrial the nation became, the number of people who could or would attend an extended camp meeting dwindled. But the idea that true religion might be cultivated by retreating temporarily from the larger society lives on, in modified form, at Sky Lake.

In time, too, the evangelical charisma exuded by the "new measures" revivalists began to weaken. As towns and cities flourished and industrial production skyrocketed, the techniques of evangelist Charles G. Finney seemed unsophisticated for a people more urbane as well as more urban. By mid-century, they were seeking a fresh alternative in the revivals of the holiness movement, initiated not by clergy but by a laywoman. The religious and cultural revitalization of the holiness revivals worked for a generation as a means to bring persons in contact with the sacred. For later generations, the revivals of evangelists such as Dwight L. Moody, Billy Sunday, and Billy Graham would play much the same role in providing a clear religious vision during times of social transition. But the perpetuation of the revival is itself a sign that the revival had become a ritual form, the enactment of which would open the doors to religious experience or reconfirm the plausibility of what had already been claimed as religious reality.

Another enduring consequence has been the stress on an inner religious experience in Methodism as a whole. Methodists have long pointed to John Wesley's heart being "strangely warmed" to appraise precisely what constitutes genuine religious experience. As a result, Methodists have minimized serious theological reflection. Looking back over two centuries of organized Methodism in the United States, one can name only a handful of individual Methodists who are noted theologians. This subordination of theology to personal religious experience has granted a doctrinal flexibility to Methodism, which contributed to its amazing growth in the nineteenth century by giving it a wide appeal. Hence, today Methodists span the theological spectrum from fundamentalist to liberal. But the elevation of experience over theology has also exacted a price, insofar as it has been virtually impossible for Methodism to articulate a consistent theological position or to speak with one voice when attempting to determine the ramifications of Christian affirmation for action in the social order.

The conversion experience fostered by camp meetings and revivals also assured that American Methodism—and most of American Protestantism—would abandon many of the views associated with the Reformation teaching of John Calvin. Again, it is Methodism's—and revivalism's—emphasis on inner experience that is largely responsible for this shift, since, as noted earlier, conversion presumes that the individual is actively involved in the process of salvation and must, through an act of the will, choose whether to accept or reject the gracious work of God. In contrast to Calvin's teaching, God alone does not decide who shall be saved. We decide for ourselves. This accent on the will also helps account for the astounding growth of Methodism in the Wyoming Conference area and elsewhere in the first half of the nineteenth century, for it was the religious approach most compatible with society at large. The prevailing cultural premise saw individual action and individual responsibility as the hallmarks of a democratic order. Through exercise of the will, men and women had transformed the frontier wilderness into civilization, were laboring to build an industrial society, and could mold the United States into the Kingdom of God on earth. Hence, those who imbibed the revival style and underwent conversion often took an active interest in social reform. If a change of the heart could make sinner into saint, so change and reform in society could transform the image of the divine Kingdom from vision to reality. But here again the cost of seeing religious experience as an inner, highly individualistic phenomenon comes to bear, for no clear blueprint for social change has emerged from private acts of the will.

Methodism in the Wyoming Conference owes much to this complex evangelical revival heritage, as does Methodism at large. The revivals not only brought large numbers of people into the Methodist fold, but they also made the experience of conversion the base for the religious life and granted to the individual control over personal destiny in religion as well as in society. If we would understand contemporary Methodism, we must be sensitive to the impact especially of the early camp meetings, the evangelical revivals of the "new measures" awakening, and the revivals generated by the holiness movement. As Francis Asbury aptly remarked in 1809, "We must attend to camp-meetings. They make our harvest times. . . ."[22]

END NOTES

1.   William G. McLoughlin, *Revivals, Awakenings, and Reform: An Essay on Religion and Social Change in America, 1607-1977,* Chicago History of American Religion Series, ed. Martin E. Marty (Chicago and London: University of Chicago Press, 1978), p. xiii.

2.   *Ibid.,* p. 2.

3.   See William James, *The Varieties of Religious Experience* [1902] (New York: Collier Books, 1961).

4.   The standard analyses of the camp meeting are Dickson D. Bruce, Jr., *And They All Sang Hallelujah: Plain-Folk Camp-Meeting Religion, 1800-1845* (Knoxville: University of Tennessee Press, 1974), and Charles A. Johnson, *The Frontier Camp Meeting: Religion's Harvest Time* (Dallas: Southern Methodist University Press, 1955).

5.   Henry Smith, *Recollections and Reflections of an Old Itinerant: A Series of Letters Originally Published in the Christian Advocate and Journal and the Western Christian Advocate,* ed. George Peck (New York: Lane & Tippett, 1848), pp. 54-55.

6.   Peter Cartwright, *Autobiography of Peter Cartwright* [1856], excerpted in *The American Evangelicals, 1800-1900,* ed. William G. McLoughlin (New York: Harper and Row, 1968). p. 47.

7.   On ritual patterns in the camp meeting, see Bruce, chapter three.

8.   My interpretation of the conversion experience, as well as that of Bruce in his study, follows Arnold van Gennep, *The Rites of Passage,* trans. Monika B. Vizedom and Gabrielle L. Chaffee (Chicago: University of Chicago Press, 1960), and Victor W. Turner, *The Ritual Process: Structure and Antistructure* (Chicago: Aldine, 1969), esp. chapter three.

9.   See Whitney R. Cross, *The Burned-Over District: The Social and Intellectual History of Enthusiastic Religion in Western New York, 1800-1850* (Ithaca: Cornell University Press, 1950).

10. George Peck, *Early Methodism Within the Bounds of the Old Genessee Conference from 1788 to 1838* (New York: Carlton & Porter, 1860), and Amasa Franklin Chaffee, *History of the Wyoming Conference of the Methodist Episcopal Church* (New York: Eaton and Mains, 1904).

11. Peck, *Early Methodism,* pp. 312-13.

12. George Peck, unpublished manuscript, George Peck Papers, George Arents Research Library, Syracuse University. I am grateful to Ms. Carolyn A. Davis, Manuscripts Librarian, and the staff of the Arents Library for permitting access to the George Peck Papers and the Wyoming Conference Papers and for the courtesies they extended to me.

13. See John William Ward, *Andrew Jackson: Symbol for an Age* (New York: Oxford University Press, 1955).

14. Along with Whitney R. Cross's study noted above, the following remain provocative studies of the social and religious tumult that marked this period: Robert T. Handy, *A Christian America: Protestant Hopes and Historical Realities* (New York: Oxford University Press, 1971); Martin E. Marty, *Righteous Empire: The Protestant Experience in America* (New York: The Dial Press, 1970); Alice Felt Tyler, *Freedom's Ferment: Phases of American Social History from the Colonial Period to the Outbreak of the Civil War* (Minneapolis: University of Minnesota Press, 1944); and Gilbert Seldes, *The Stammering Century* [1928] (Gloucester, MA: Peter Smith, 1972).

15. On Finney and the genesis of modern evangelical revivalism, see Charles G. Finney, *Memoirs of Rev. Charles G. Finney* (New York: A. S. Barnes, 1976); William G. McLoughlin, *Modern Revivalism* (New York: Ronald Press, 1959); his *Revivals, Awakenings, and Reform,* chapter four; Bernard A. Weisberger, *They Gathered at the River: The Story of the Great Revivalists and Their Impact upon Religion in America* (Boston: Little, Brown and Co., 1958); and Cross's study noted above.

16. Charles G. Finney, *Lectures on Revivals of Religion* (New York: Leavitt, Lord & Co., 1835).

17. On the surge of Methodism in this period, see Elizabeth Nottingham, *Methodism and the Frontier* (New York: Columbia University Press, 1944); Emory S. Bucke, ed., *History of American Methodism,* 3 vols. (Nashville: Abingdon Press, 1964); and the many studies of William Warren Sweet.

18. On this point, see Nathan O. Hatch's provocative essay, *"Sola Scriptura and Novus Ordo Seclorum,"* in *The Bible in America: Essays in Cultural History,* ed. Nathan O. Hatch and Mark A. Noll (New York: Oxford University Press, 1982), pp. 59-78.

19. The classic analysis of this movement remains Timothy L. Smith, *Revivalism and Social Reform: American Protestantism on the Eve of the Civil War* (Nashville: Abingdon Press, 1957).

20. Finney, *Memoirs,* pp. 350-51.

21. I am grateful to Mrs. Grace Terwilliger for sharing with me a copy of her brief history of the Sidney Grove camp meeting.

22. Quoted in Johnson, title page.

GEORGE PECK

Edgar Singer

Although upstate New York in the late 1700's was rapidly losing its frontier aspect, it was still a land of broad virgin forest, with roads that were often nothing more than winding paths through the trees. Much of the travel was by horseback, and Luther Peck, the blacksmith, found ready employment for his skills. He, together with his wife and children, had moved to Middlefield, New York in 1794, coming from Danbury, Connecticut, erecting a log cabin home and a blacksmith shop. Amid these primitive surroundings, young George was born on August 8, 1797, the youngest of 10 children. All 5 of the boys became Methodist circuit riders, with one of them, Jesse, being elected to the episcopacy. But they had many disadvantages to overcome, chiefly their sketchy education, obtained in the village school, where the instruction was inadequate and the punishment "barbarous." But the children learned to read, and all of them took part in the book readings which occurred in the evenings whenever a volume of particular interest was secured. The whole family participated in the lively discussion, and George grew up with the conviction that books were sources of excitement and pleasure. He never outgrew his love for reading. Down through the years he educated himself by a disciplinary program of critical study. Except for one contact with a class in Hebrew at the Auburn Theological School, he never attended any educational institution, except for those reluctant hours in the little school in Middlefield. Nevertheless he became an influential member of his Conference, the Genessee, which in those days took in all of the territory of the present Wyoming Conference, together with territory north into Canada and as far west as Detroit. He had the unusual distinction of being elected to the General Conference for 13 consecutive sessions—a total of 52 years. For 12 years he served as editor of church periodicals and acted as general book editor of the publishing house.

The family into which George Peck was born was not a church-attending one, but an experience involving a vivid dream of impending death motivated the father to be more open to the preaching of the Methodist circuit riders. Eventually they all joined the Methodist society. As for himself, George always felt that his religious life took on a new dimension when, in a solitary moment, he experienced the forgiving grace of God, November 12, 1812. Surrounded by religious influences in the family and with circuit riders as regular visitors in the home, George grew to be a young man who liked to assist in the services and take leadership in the church. When the preacher, Loring Grant, invited him to accompany him on a month-long tour around the circuit, he eagerly accepted. At the conclusion of this introduction to the preaching life, he and Grant called on the presiding elder and asked for a permanent assignment. Peck was appointed to be Grant's assistant until the Annual Conference, without pay. The year was 1816 and Peck was 19.

The two of them resolved to hold a camp meeting that same summer, to begin on July 4th. They secured a site in Plymouth and worked hard in the woods to prepare the ground. The brush was cleared and a fence of discarded branches placed around the place. Notices were sent out far and wide, and one of the bishops, William McKendree, secured as the featured preacher. A crowd assembled. The bishop, a striking figure of a man, delivered what Peck felt was a "great sermon." But, even with the bishop's eloquence, the crowd seemed unmoved. It was left to Timothy Dewey, commonly called "Father Dewey," to save the day. He preached a "terrific sermon on the words, 'Prepare to meet thy God.' " His voice was "terrible as thunder" as he called out, "O sinner, sinner, are you determined to take hell by storm? . . . Are your bones iron, and your flesh brass, that you plunge headlong into the lake of fire?"[1] A great commotion arose all over the camp. Seekers were invited to come forward for prayer, and many were converted. The meeting went on all night.

This was the first of many such events that Peck helped to plan and conduct. He was always a zealous supporter of the camp meeting movement and believed, even with due acknowledgment of the excessive quality of the "jumpings" and other violent manifestations of religious excitement, that the church possessed an important resource in those meetings in the forest.

The Methodists of those days were an emotional and shouting fellowship, with emphasis on "vital religion," as opposed, perhaps, to lukewarm or merely formal faith. The preachers affirmed that all those who had not experienced a positive experience of God's forgiving grace were certain to be consigned to eternal punishment in the final judgment. When, therefore, worshipers came to a feeling of forgiveness and certainty, sensing that God had looked with favor upon them, they were ready to explode with joy and relief. A common question among the Christian people was, "How do you feel?" The assumption was that if a person felt forgiven, then, indeed, he or she was forgiven. The Methodist meetings were characterized by heartfelt singing, impassioned prayers, and forthright preaching. Peck was unhesitatingly a participant in this religious scene, even though he was aware that his own solitary experience of forgiveness was somewhat less emotional and soul-wrenching than he had been led to expect. For years he longed for what he termed a "clearer vision" which would remove all doubt and uncertainty. Eventually he was rewarded, it would seem, when he was 42, again in a solitary place, in an experience of the wonder of God's grace. From that time onward he felt a new spiritual freedom and sensed that he was held in God's protecting power.

Following the camp meeting mentioned above, Peck went to the Conference session and was appointed, according to the custom of the time for fledgling preachers, as an assistant to a regular circuit rider, Elisha Bibbens, and sent to the Broome Circuit. As soon as possible he set out to make his first tour of duty throughout the preaching places. There were 28 of them, mostly private homes, with congregations as small as 6 persons, 366 members in all. In the fashion of all Methodist preachers of the time, bishops included, he ate his meals with Methodist families, slept in their cabins or out in the barn with the animals, and rode his horse during the day to the next appointment. It was a life of rigor and discomfort. At one log cabin where he stopped, there was noting to eat, and he and the housewife had to wait patiently until the husband came in from the hunt, bearing a freshly-slain deer. The roads were nearly non-existent. Once he had to engage a boy as a guide to lead him to the next scheduled stop, one near Hawleyton, the people assuring him that he would never be able to find his way alone through the forest. But he had interesting experiences as well. Up the river from Great Bend he stopped in with Jesse H. Hale, whose daughter was later married to the Mormon prophet, Joseph Smith. Hale, in the years to come, would regale him with stories of Smith, whom he considered a great imposter.

Perhaps the greatest danger he ran into, as did most of the other circuit riders, was that of recurring and severe illness. The fatigue of constant riding, the exposure to wind and rain, and the often tainted food, brought on bouts with vaguely-diagnosed illnesses for which there was no treatment except the home remedies of the people. More than once he despaired of his life. But he persevered and lived on into old age. Many of his contemporaries were less fortunate.

After 5 years on the circuits, changing his assignment each year, as was the rule, he was appointed to one of the few "station" charges in the Conference, Sauquoit, N. Y. This was an unusual honor for one so new in the ministry. It seems that the Conference was meeting in that church, and Peck had been invited to preach at one of the open air services, held in the evening. The bishop, Enoch George, was present and was evidently much impressed with the young preacher, for he appointed him to that church the first thing the next morning. Although he had found that riding the circuit was hard enough, he discovered that serving a single church was almost more demanding. He now had to prepare 3 different sermons each week, including a prayer meeting talk, instead of being able to preach the same sermon 28 times during the month. But his habits of study during the previous years stood him in good stead. He had amassed a fund of material for his sermons, and enjoyed the work of putting his talks together.

He was already, at 25, recognized as a person of intelligence and force. From the first he had been studying Wesley's *Sermons* and Fletcher's *Checks to Antinomianism,* both standard fare for a Methodist preacher, but he was steadily branching further afield. A typical report is instructive:

"My plans of study, whether wise or otherwise, were definite and laborious. I now had access to Clark's Commentary on the Historical Books of the Old Testament, Dr. Scott's Notes on the Prophets, and Dr. Coke's Commentary on the New Testament. I began all these authors at once, reading a chapter in each, with the notes, every day, and completed them during the year. To this I added a regular course of history, which included the works of Prideaux and Harmer."[2]

Soon he was reading philosophy and delving into the religious and literary life of Great Britain.

He was also being drawn into the dominant controversies of the time, especially the one having to do with the presiding elder question. America was going through a time of re-evaluation of its spirit and practice, especially in the field of government. There had been, in the past, a strong aristocratic tinge to society, with the great landholders of Colonial days exerting an immense amount of power and influence. But the common people were now beginning to assert themselves. They seized upon Andrew Jackson as the symbol of the new order and elected him President in 1829. Within the church, the same problems were being faced. The church of John Wesley and Francis Asbury had never been a particularly democratic institution, and that of the 1820's continued the same pattern. Bishops held autocratic power, and the presiding elders, appointed by them and responsible solely to them, were ready targets. Circuit riders had no voice in their assignment, nor were lay men and women consulted about church government. The party promoting the new point of view, advocating the election of presiding elders in the Annual Conference and the sending of laity to the General Conference, called themselves "The Reformers." They published a magazine setting forth their views. Peck joined their number. When the time came for the Annual Conference to elect delegates to the General Conference, so popular had the Reformers become, that all those elected were of this persuasion. Peck was included, the youngest of the group.

At the General Conference in Baltimore he sat back and listened while others took up the cause. A heated debate arose, with loud complaints against the bishops and presiding elders, but in the end the reform party was defeated. When he got home, Peck had to face the question of how far he was going to continue in his support of this agitation. Some of its leaders seemed to be saying that if the church would not change, they were going to have to leave it. Within 6 years, the break did come, and the Methodist Protestant Church was formed, embodying the ideals of the reformers. But Peck never went this far. He was, perhaps in the best sense of the word, an "organization man," or a committed church man. He felt that the business of the church was to save souls and that it must be preserved in unity to perform this task. When he discovered that the church as a whole was not going to adopt the program of the reformers, he withdrew from the movement.

He returned from the General Conference to give himself wholeheartedly to the work at home. A proposal was in hand from the trustees of the church at Cazenovia to establish a school in their old church building, if the Conference would adopt it and make it the Conference school. This was a daring proposal, because the history of Methodist schools in this country was not a particularly happy one. All those previously established, including Cokesbury College, had, for one reason or another, closed their doors or were struggling along in a precarious existence. The proposal was referred to the Committee on Education, of which Peck was the chairman. After much discussion, the plan was approved, and Peck was delegated to present it to the Conference. The result of the Conference action was that

Cazenovia Seminary was opened later that same year as a school for both sexes. Co-education was very much a debated subject in those days, but the school prospered.

Peck always was ready to support educational development. It was reported, years later, that he was the moving influence behind the decision of the General Conference to establish a course of study for ordained ministers. (It already had such a course for ministers on trial.) He was an eager advocate of the proposal to found Wyoming Seminary, and always took credit for proposing the idea. He served as Principal of Cazenovia Seminary for 4 years. And when the ill-fated Conference Seminary in Binghamton came into financial straits, he was summoned by the trustees to join their number and see what could be done to save the school. During these years, a number of schools and colleges were established in the church, and Peck could be counted upon to speak for them, using his powers of persuasion to silence the critics who feared "too much education." It is to be remembered that the Methodist Episcopal Church had not always been a strong advocate for the schools. The *Discipline* of 1784 advised preachers not to permit study and learning to interfere with soul-saving: "If you can do but one, let your studies alone. We would throw by all the libraries in the world rather than be guilty of the loss of one soul."[3] Peck was one of the new breed of preachers who believed that learning and vital piety could go together, even as Wesley did.

But this was to come later. For the moment, he was faced with the responsibilities of being a presiding elder, having been named to that post by Bishop Enoch George in spite of the fact that he was known as a member of the Reform party. At first he was not sure he was mature enough or experienced enough to succeed at his task, but he found that the other clergy accepted him readily. He was assigned to the Susquehanna District, which took in most of what is now known as the Wyoming Conference. It had 11 "charges" or circuits and 3,696 members. As presiding elder he was expected to visit each charge 4 times a year to conduct the Quarterly Meetings. These weekend sessions were intended for the entire circuit and would draw people from as many as 28 preaching places. The meetings provided opportunities for spiritual refreshment and social contact for the people isolated in their little hamlets. The sessions began on Saturday mornings, usually, with a prayer meeting, to be followed by a business meeting. A second prayer meeting concluded the day. Sunday morning was a time for a Love Feast, a service of testimony, prayer and singing, closed to all but members. These services, lasting up to 3 hours, frequently used an "agape" or love meal of bread, perhaps with water. In these Love Feasts the Methodist people could bring their faith to a bright glow again after the discouragements of the intervening months. The Sunday observance continued with a preaching service, after which the people left in the afternoon to make their way home. Peck would often be away for as long as 6 weeks at a time, conducting these quarterly events.

One of the responsibilities of the presiding elder was to see to it that Methodist books were sold in every circuit. He worked through the preachers, who were the chief salesmen and who were allowed to keep a small commission from their sales. They were also the bookkeepers in the transactions. Often people could pay only a small portion of the purchase price at any one time and had to be carried along for months at a time. Such book promotion was characteristic of the entire Methodist Episcopal Church. The result of this painstaking attention to religious literature was an education among the people in the things of the faith that fostered unity among the congregations. It might be said that the camp meetings were at one pole in the church's outreach and program, with their emotionalism and mass appeal, but the more disciplined and thoughtful reading program was at the other.

An additional educational resource was the Sunday School. It is commonly stated that this movement began in 1780 in Gloucester, England, but it ought to be remembered that 32 years before that, in the same city, the Methodist Conference authorized the formation of children's societies for religious instruction. The two traditions evidently reinforced each other, and by 1786, Sunday Schools were being established among American Methodists. The Methodist Sunday School Union was formed in 1827, and 17 years later, upon Peck's earnest advocacy, an editor was named for the Sunday School literature of the church. It is interesting to note that Peck's motion in the General Conference was opposed by the eminent Dr. Nathan Bangs, on the ground that it would involve needless expense. However, the measure passed, and the first editor was appointed, thus beginning a long history of professional oversight for the church's literature for children, youth and adults.

While he was presiding elder of the Susquehanna District, he became involved in controversy with the Rev. C. R. Marsh, Universalist paster in Hop Bottom, Pa. This individual had begun publishing a magazine entitled "The Candid Examiner" and had included in it an attack on the "limitarians," as he termed them, the more orthodox Christians whose theology limited eternal salvation to those who had faith in Christ. Marsh offered to print the reply of anyone who cared to answer. This came to Peck's attention and he responded in 5 articles, setting forth the Methodist view as he understood it. The magazine ceased publication before all the articles were published, but Peck was now before the public in a new way. He went on to publish his first book *Universalism Examined* (1827). He lost money on the project and remarked wryly that "it is possible that writing the book was a greater benefit to me than reading it has been to anyone else."[4]

Meanwhile, the country was filling up with people, and it seemed to many that the Genessee Conference was simply too large for effective administration. (The churches in Canada had been grouped into a separate Conference in 1824.) A petition was sent to the General Conference of 1828, asking for the formation of a new Conference, the Oneida, out of the old Genessee. In supporting this motion, Peck was warmly opposed by those from the West and South who saw in this an opening to a kind of Congregationalism in church government as over against Methodist connectionalism. However, the measure passed, and the new Conference met a Cazenovia the next year. By this time, Peck had concluded a one year pastorate at Ithaca and went on to short pastorates at Utica, Cazenovia and Auburn. While at Utica, he was again sent to the General Conference (1832) and there heard Dr. William Capers of South Carolina decline the office of bishop, on the grounds that he was, from necessity, not from choice, a slaveholder, and felt that as such he could not serve the whole church effectively, especially in the North. He suggested the name of James O. Andrew of Georgia, who did not own any slaves. Andrew was elected. It was this same Bishop Andrew who, in 1844, by that time a slaveholder, precipitated the agonized debate that rent the church asunder, North and South.

It was while he was at Auburn that Peck conceived the idea of a project of writing several small books to embrace the lives of the apostles and their immediate successors, using material from Eusebius and other ancient historians. The book editor of the church favored the plan, and the first volume, *Lives of the Apostles and Evangelists,* was completed and published. The project, however, was not continued. Illness and extreme fatigue overcame Peck, as it had before.

One event at Auburn reflects the religious and community situation of the time. Peck was conducting a series of special meetings and revival services. On one occasion he invited those who desired special prayers for themselves to come forward. Some 20 young men of the town who had come to church that night as a joke walked to the front of the church, but, instead of bowing in prayer, they laughed to each other and made slighting remarks about the minister. They refused to leave. Finally, in desperation, Peck had to send for the police, who cleared them from the building.

It was at the Oneida Conference of 1834 that he delivered a major address on the subject of the proposed theological seminaries. There were many who opposed such a development, fearing, among other things, that such a move would draw needed support away from the newly-established colleges. The substance of Peck's address, in which he advocated the establishment of theological schools, was published in the "Methodist Quarterly Review and Magazine" for 1836. He lived to see his line of argument adopted by the General Conference. Although he was not the only one in favor of such theological education, and perhaps not the foremost leader, yet his support was crucial for the eventual founding of Drew Theological Seminary in 1866. In recounting his part in this, he said, with characteristic humor, "I name these facts, not through ostentation, but hoping that my being at one time 20 years ahead of the age may be pleaded in mitigation of the offense, if I should at any time be convicted of falling behind it."[5]

In 1835 he was elected Principal of Cazenovia Seminary, now 10 years old, a position he was to hold for 4 years. Upon his election, his friend, Wilbur Fisk, President of Wesleyan University, now in its third year of existence, conferred on him the honorary degree of Master of Arts. This was significant not only in itself, but because it indicated the position that Peck was assuming among the leaders of the church, especially in its educational endeavors. While at Cazenovia, in addition to his administrative duties, he taught Hebrew, philosophy, logic and rhetoric, subjects which, with the exception of Hebrew, he had pretty much learned by himself. Here again, as at

Auburn, he had to contend with blatantly irreligious young men. One of them read a paper in one of the classes that Peck felt was designed to bring revivals and religion into contempt. He expelled the student the next day.

At the General Conference of 1836, in Cincinnati, the slavery issue came to the fore when two of the delegates, Orange Scott and George Storrs, both of Massachusetts, attended an abolition meeting one evening and appeared on the program. This incensed a number of the delegates, who were bitterly opposed to the entire abolition movement, and a resolution was passed censuring the two for their presumption. One of the delegates referred to "the length and breadth of their damning iniquity." Peck felt the motion to censure was too pro-slavery and voted against it, but it passed overwhelmingly.

Abolitionists believed that slavery was a thoroughly evil system and that the church ought to separate itself from that institution at once and completely. Peck, though no defender of slavery, could not bring himself to believe that it is always a sin to own slaves. He supported other methods to "ameliorate" the slaves' condition, programs which might hold out hope of keeping the church from splitting on this issue. The issue surfaced in the Oneida Conference within a few weeks, when the same two men, Scott and Storrs, came to Cortlandville where the Conference was meeting and arranged to give lectures each afternoon on the subject of "Slavery and the Church." Although he had not wanted to censure the two men earlier, Peck now offered a resolution in Conference to the effect that the action of these Abolitionists was "irregular and intrusive." Peck's motion passed, and the two abolitionists left town. Perhaps he felt that by eliminating the influence of Storrs and Scott, the violent passions connected with the abolitionist movement could be kept out of the Oneida Conference.

At the General Conference of 1840 Peck was made secretary of the church-wide Committee on Slavery. The Committee met almost daily, in an effort to find some sort of compromise, but could not come to any agreement. One of the side issues that came before the Conference was whether the testimony of black church members could be admitted in church trials in those states where such testimony was not allowed in courts of law. Peck, concerned to "save" the South, spoke in favor of a resolution that would have denied this right. The motion passed. Immediately he found himself in the middle of a highly charged controversy. Black Methodist churches responded immediately with remonstrances; Peck's friends were distressed. Within a few days he arose to move reconsideration of the resolution, but his motion was lost. Peck was forced to bear the obloquy of this act.

Even with all this, a great and sobering honor came to him. At this same General Conference, he was elected editor of the "Methodist Quarterly Review" and book editor of the publishing house. He immediately moved his family to New York City and joined the New York Annual Conference. He was caught up in a whirlwind of activities, which included not only his work as editor but also his duties as something of a spokesman for the church. Following an attack by an Episcopalian, he wrote 16 articles for the "Christian Advocate" in defense of the Methodist church. Within 2 years he published two books, *Scripture Doctrine of Christian Perfection* and *Rule of Faith*.

The General Conference of 1844 drew near, and Peck was again elected to its membership. He was made chairman of the Committee on Slavery and was in the midst of the controversy over Bishop James O. Andrew. In the end, a Plan of Separation was adopted, making possible the establishment of two sister Methodist denominations, North and South. Peck had hoped that, if the Southern Conferences actually went on to form a separate denomination, a spirit of friendliness and mutuality might prevail; he was dismayed at the bitterness displayed. When Henry B. Bascom of Virginia published vitriolic condemnations of the Northern church, Peck was asked to reply, which he did in a book of 160 pages under the title *Slavery and the Episcopacy*. And when in 1848 the thorny question of the division of the assets of the publishing house between the two churches had to be faced, Peck was one of the 3 Commissioners named to represent the M. E. Church.

In 1848, he was elected editor of the *New York Christian Advocate*, the influential Methodist weekly. He resolved to use the paper as a means of healing the divisions in the church, "to close the old controversies, and make the paper minister, as far as possible, to the peace of the church."[6] He kept his word. For 4 years, while controversy concerning slavery raged throughout the country, the pages of the "Advocate" reflected none of it. He was castigated as one who was afraid to speak his mind and denounced as a temporizer, but he refused to change his position. At the end of the 4 years, he returned to the pastorate. Perhaps he was eased out of office because he seemed to be insensitive to the moral questions of his time.

He joined again the Conference of his youth, now the Wyoming Conference, formed by a division of the Oneida Conference, meeting for its first session in Carbondale, Pa. in 1852. He was welcomed into its ranks and asked to represent the church in an unpleasant heresy trial. He won the case. From 1852 to his retirement in 1873, he served as pastor and presiding elder within the Conference. He continued to publish his books, including *Wyoming, Early Methodism,* and his fascinating *Life and Times of George Peck* (1874). He continued as a part-time editor for the publishing house, managed to be disliked enough in the South to be denounced at a mock funeral for him held in Richmond, Virginia, and ended his days, respected by a wide host of those who honored him for having tried to steer a middle course in a time when such seemed impossible.

END NOTES

1.   George Peck, *The Life and Times of George Peck, D. D.* (New York: Nelson and Phillips, 1874), p. 64.

2.   *Ibid.,* p. 124.

3.   William Warren Sweet, *Methodism in American History* (New York: Abingdon Press, 1954), p. 223.

4.   Peck, *The Life and Times of George Peck, D. D.,* p. 152.

5.   *Ibid.,* p. 207.

6.   *Ibid.,* p. 322.

ADDITIONAL WORKS CONSULTED

1. Leroy E. Bugbee, *He Holds the Stars in His Hands*. Wyoming Conference, 1952.

2. A. F. Chaffee, *History of the Wyoming Conference of the Methodist Episcopal Church*. New York: Eaton and Mains, 1904.

3. Charles Elliott, *History of the Great Secession from the Methodist Episcopal Church in the Year 1845*. Cincinnati: Swormstedt and Poe, 1855.

4. *Christian Advocate*. New York: 1850.

5. *Journal of the General Conference*, 1840.

6. *Journal of the General Conference*, 1844.

7. *Methodist Quarterly Review*, 1840.

8. Frederick A. Norwood (ed.), *Sourcebook of American Methodism*. Nashville: Abingdon, 1982.

9. George Peck, *A Short Account of the Life of George Peck*. Manuscript, 1813.

10. George Peck, *George Pecks [sic] Life Scribbled by Himself*. Undated manuscript.

11. George Peck, D. D., *Slavery and the Episcopacy*. New York: G. Lane and C. P. Tippett, 1845.

12. George Peck, D. D., *The Past and the Present, A Semi-Centennial Sermon*. New York: Carlton and Porter, 1866.

13. J. K. Peck, A. M., *Luther Peck and His Five Sons*. New York: Eaton and Mains, 1897.

14. William Warren Sweet, *Methodism in American History*. New York: Abingdon, 1954.

15. William Warren Sweet, *Religion on the American Frontier: Volume IV, The Methodists*. Chicago: University of Chicago Press, 1946.

JOSEPH SMITH IN SUSQUEHANNA COUNTRY: MORMON BEGINNINGS

John Goodell

The *Book of Mormon* was published in 1830. It was presented as the translation of a series of golden tablets found by Joseph Smith, at the direction of the angel Moroni, buried in a hill near Palmyra, New York. Much of the human drama of Joseph Smith in the formative days of Mormonism, as well as the "translation" of the *Book of Mormon,* took place within the boundaries of the present Wyoming Conference—at Afton and Colesville, New York, and at Harmony, Pennsylvania, near Lanesboro. Along with these geographical connections, there are some significant and interesting ways in which Joseph Smith had contact with Methodism and Methodists.

Most Methodists today have heard of the Mormon Church, the Church of Jesus Christ of the Latter Day Saints (LDS), but few know much about it. If we know anything at all, we probably have heard that they place an emphasis on family, they are conservative on the issue of women's roles (anti-ERA), they are committed tithers, and they do a good job of taking care of their own but do not reach out to non-Mormons, except to make them converts. All of those issues are rooted in an early history that enshrined nineteenth-century evangelical values in a body of revelation centered in the *Book of Mormon.* Many of the same dynamics that contributed to the growth of Methodism in this area of New York and Pennsylvania also helped launch Mormonism on its long and fascinating history. In the following pages, we will examine some of those dynamics and look at many of those early events from the life of Joseph Smith that are also a part of the local history of churches and communities within the Wyoming Conference.

The period after the War for Independence and the making of the Constitution was marked by emigration West from the eastern seaboard. It was a time of new opportunity coming on the heels of often dire economic hardships occasioned by the years of war. There were great dreams of a new nation, of new community, of a continuing revival that would eventually result in the coming of the Kingdom of God on earth. These dreams were a source of ferment, of creativity, and of great energy. But they also meant that people began to migrate to places of greater opportunity. As people moved, communities, families, and church ties were upset. Loyalties to community and church were broken and forged anew. This creativity and ferment gave rise to religious renewal, which, in turn, generated conflict that was frequently intense. Joseph Smith found himself at the center of all these dynamics.

Many of the early migrations from New England came directly through portions of what was to become Wyoming Conference. Place names like Norwich, Guilford, and New Milford testify to the coming of settlers from towns of the same name in Connecticut, Vermont, and other New England states. Much of the main thrust of that migration and early development came along the route of the Erie Canal, but the area affected extended in all directions.[1] Commercial connections to the Erie Canal were common, an example of which was the Chenango Canal, which came down to Binghamton from Utica.

Along with the migrations came the revivals. The flux and turmoil of new communities made upper New York State a fertile ground for the seeds of the Spirit. There were frequent and comprehensive waves of revival that coursed through virtually all of the communities in that section—in the winter of 1799-1800, in 1807-8, after the War of 1812, and into the 1820's. It is reported that the Methodists alone gained 16 percent in 1818.[2] It is no wonder that Western New York came to be called the Burned-Over District, as the flames of revival burned over the land.

Careful examination of church records reveals the existence of many Methodist class meetings that date from this period. We know that South Bainbridge (now Afton) was placed on a circuit in 1820.[3] There was a class at East Windsor, not too far from Colesville, by 1812, as well as one at Harmony, Pennsylvania. Though Great Bend does not figure directly into this story, we know that Methodism was there at least by 1799.[4] That location is probably less than ten miles from where Joseph Smith was to live for a time.

It is always interesting to wonder what people back then were like. Who were these people who settled the land, land not always better than what they had left in rocky New England? I like to imagine that many of the present older residents of our rural areas offer important clues. Some of them still live on the land settled by their forebears 180 years or more ago. They tend to be practical, tough, hard-working, and strongly individualistic. They speak their thoughts directly, often with a cutting wit. Among this population is a powerful democratic spirit, with little respect for professional classes or for anyone who would think him- or herself better than others. Religion, therefore, should be practical and down-to-earth, and be clear-cut and reasonable. All of this was part of the world of Joseph Smith and of the rise of Mormonism.

As we trace the events in his early life, it is important to keep in mind that much of our information was written down after Joseph Smith became the Mormon prophet. At points, it might have been subject to some embellishment. There is also a great deal of legend concerning him, which tends to be either very uncritical or very hostile. The basic turning points of the story are, however, fairly clear.

Joseph Smith, Jr., our Joseph, was born December 23, 1805 in Sharon, Vermont. He was preceded by 150 years of ancestors in New England on his father's side and a line of Scottish clergy on his mother's side. In that history were both religious passion and individualistic non-conformity. Those forebears sought to keep the integrity of their own religious experience, and especially Joseph, Sr., was contemptuous of established churches. His wife Lucy was excited by Methodist revivals in Vermont in 1810, but he was further convinced "that there was no order or class of religionists that know any more concerning the kingdom of God than those of the world."[5] Joseph, Sr. was himself subject to dreams or visions that were an important part of his religious experience. They were later described in Lucy's biography of her famous son.[6] There apparently was an atmosphere of religious devotion in the home, as religion, faith, and Bible reading were continuing concerns, with their life being touched from time to time by revivals.

The material fortunes of the Smith family waxed and waned. After a series of difficulties, Joseph, Sr. moved his family to Manchester, near Palmyra, New York, in 1816. At the time, Palmyra was a thriving town of about 4000 people. Here they were exposed to democratic revivalism in the raw, as a series of Methodist exhorters and other revival preachers passed through the community. In later years, Joseph, in looking back on this period, reported that he "caught a spark of Methodist fire" at a camp meeting in the woods on the Vienna road. He considered joining the Methodist church for a time, but decided, true to his heritage, that neither the Methodists nor anyone else was quite right. Still, it was not uncommon for him to be found at a Methodist camp meeting. At that time, such camp meetings were normally scheduled at regular intervals to coincide with the passing through of the circuit rider. Joseph was so frequent an attender that he was often asked to be an "exhorter" at these meetings.[7]

Somewhere around 1820, Joseph apparently had a religious experience of some kind. He reported it in retrospect in 1832 and again in 1838—both times after the Mormon Church had been launched. He described a sense of being surrounded by a thick darkness which was penetrated by a pillar of light. Two figures appeared to him, one of which was apparently Jesus, who told Joseph that all of the sects (religious denominations) were wrong and their professors corrupt.[8] Our prophet-to-be described that whole sequence as an overpowering vision. Joseph said that he recounted his vision to one of the Methodist preachers involved in the revivals. The preacher reacted with contempt, telling Joseph that his vision had come from the devil. Joseph's later reports of the incident indicate that he was hurt by the reaction.[9] They also served to support his feeling that even the best of the religious sects was mistaken. Again, there are no accounts of this early experience written anywhere near the time it happened.

It was not long after this that Joseph began a train of events that led his history to overlap with that of several of the communities that are now in the Wyoming Conference. Like many of his time, Joseph was something of a dreamer and adventurer. We have already recounted some evidence of his lively imagination. He was also a treasure hunter. In a time when there seemed to be a new opportunity at every turn of events and every uncovering of new landscape, there was a market for persons who could aid in the finding of fortune. One common method for finding treasure was the seer stone, or "peeping" stone. Certain stones of various descriptions, usually uncommon, were reputed to give sensitive owners the power to see where buried treasure was located. One owner of such a stone was Joseph Smith, Jr.

There are several accounts concerning Joseph and his seer stone. One has it that he discovered it when he was digging a well for Mason Chase. The report said that he found it twenty-four feet underground and that with it he could see "ghosts, infernal spirits, mountains of gold and silver."[10] There are several hearsay reports of his peeping stone which tend to differ from one another. There may indeed have been several of them. He used them, or it, to help neighbors look for buried treasure. Some of the tales about his exploits include a measure of necromancy. One neighbor testified that Joseph told him there was buried treasure on his land. They took a black sheep to the spot and led it around a circle with its throat bleeding in order to appease the evil spirit guarding the treasure. The procedure did not work. Joseph's explanation was that there was a mistake made in the process of killing the sheep.[11]

Years later, Joseph admitted that he had been a money-digger but that it was not particularly profitable. He denied involvement in the more exotic rituals attributed to him. According to Brigham Young, the leader of the church as it moved West in the 1850's, Joseph said in 1841, "every man who lived on the earth is entitled to a seer stone, and should have one, but they are kept from them in consequence of their wickedness."[12] Seer stones were deeply valued by Joseph throughout his life, for it was on such stones that his destiny turned.

Josiah Stowell (or Stoal) of South Bainbridge (Afton) had heard of the remarkable young man with the stone and went to the Smith family home at Manchester. Stowell claimed to have a map of a lost silver mine dating from the time of Spanish explorations in the Susquehanna Valley in Northeastern Pennsylvania. He wanted to hire Joseph and some helpers to assist him in finding the mine. Joseph took his father and several others and accompanied Stowell to Harmony Township, Pennsylvania, where they boarded with Isaac and Elizabeth Hale near the supposed site of the mine.

In the Hales, Joseph crossed paths with Methodists once again. Along with many others, this staunchly Methodist family came from Vermont sometime after 1785. Their homestead was about six miles above Great Bend.[13] Isaac was a skillful hunter and took long trips up Starucca Creek to shoot elk. He would salt the meat and bring it home, leaving some at the door of the needy.[14] The Hales often housed the itinerating Methodist preachers of the Broome County circuit, and they may well have been among the first Methodists in the area. There was reportedly a class in Harmony as early as 1812. Meetings were held in houses in the winter, in barns in the summer. Later there were meetings in the log schoolhouse at Lanesboro, which was organized as a church in 1834.[15] It is not clear whether this later church was the direct successor to the Hales' earlier meetings. George Peck, an early circuit rider in the area, spoke of Isaac as "Father Hale" and commented upon his hunting skill. Peck mentioned preaching in a log schoolhouse to "a small but earnest congregation" at Harmony.[16]

The year was 1825. Joseph Smith, Jr. was a handsome young man. The Hales had a pretty daughter, Emma, aged 21. They seem to have been immediately attracted to one another. Her admiration of the young man was not shared by her father. At first Isaac even helped finance the treasure search, but he rapidly became disillusioned. As he wrote later, "Young Smith gave the 'money-diggers' great encouragement, at first, but when they had arrived in digging to near the place where he had stated an immense treasure would be found—he said the enchantment was so powerful that he could not see. They then became discouraged, and soon after dispersed."[17]

In November of that year, Joseph's father returned to Palmyra, but Joseph remained on the farm of Josiah Stowell near South Bainbridge. Stowell was a "Vermont sufferer," a reference perhaps to the hardships of trying to farm in Vermont. He established a farm two miles below South Bainbridge on the banks of the Susquehanna. Stowell was a respected member of the community with grown children, and he was a deacon in the local Presbyterian Church.[18] Apparently he never stopped believing in Joseph. While there, Joseph worked, attended school, hunted for treasure, and took expeditions down to Harmony to visit Emma Hale, to her father's dismay. All was going well for young Joseph.

Then he crossed paths with another Methodist. There resulted an event that has remained an embarrassment to the Mormon Church to this day. Peter Bridgeman was an ardent young twenty-two-year-old Methodist and a nephew of Josiah Stowell. He became concerned seeing so much of his uncle's money going into the pocket of the young glass-looker. Out of concern to protect the family welfare, and possibly out of zeal to remove moral evil, he swore out a warrant against Joseph on the charge of his being a disorderly person and an imposter. A bill found in the Chenango County Courthouse in Norwich refers to the trial of "Joseph Smith The Glass Looker" on March 20, 1826, for a misdemeanor.

The trial took place in Bainbridge, probably South Bainbridge, before a justice of the peace. Many witnesses were called to the stand, including Joseph himself. In the earliest known account of the trial, Joseph admitted that he had a certain stone that he occasionally used to search for hidden treasures and lost property, but that he had pretty much given it up because of the strain on his eyes from looking into the stone. Then others, including Stowell, also testified. He was found guilty, but there is no record of his being sentenced, perhaps because he was a minor.[19] He may have learned a lesson, for there is no more evidence of treasure seeking, though Joseph was by no means finished with seer stones.

Peter Bridgeman disappears from the story of Joseph Smith, but a month after the trial, this young Methodist was given an exhorter's license. Two years later he received his local preacher's license, and in 1832 he was ordained local deacon. Bridgeman was a member of the class meeting at West Bainbridge (North Afton) and was active in its incorporation in 1829 as "The Society of the Methodist Episcopal Church and congregation in Newton Hollow." They became the West Bainbridge Methodist Episcopal Church in 1833 and eventually the North Afton M.E. Church. When Peter

Bridgeman died in 1872, his fellow ministers characterized him as "an ardent Methodist and any attack upon either the doctrines or the polity of the M. E. Church, within his field of labor, was sure to be repelled by him with a vigorous hand."[20] His zeal, born of an early conversion, perhaps at the hand of a circuit rider, was characteristic of this time of revivals. It was not unlike the zeal of later followers of the Mormon prophet.

Joseph continued to live and work with Josiah Stowell for several months. He was not welcome at the Hale house, but he found ways to continue to visit Emma when her father was out hunting. In November, 1826, Joseph left Stowell and went to work for his family's old friend, Joseph Knight, Jr. of Colesville, a location much closer to Harmony. Knight furnished him with horse and buggy to visit Emma. When Joseph asked Isaac Hale for his daughter's hand, he was refused. There are a couple of accounts of events that led to the wedding. In one account Stowell invited Emma to visit Joseph at his house. In another, Joseph rode to Harmony and was seen riding out of town with Emma behind him while her parents were in church.[21] In any case, they were married on January 18, 1827, at the home of Squire Tarbell of South Bainbridge. Today, a marker stands near the spot where the house used to be, at the site of the present Afton Fairgrounds.

After the ceremony they departed for Manchester to live with Joseph's parents. Eight months later, they got up their courage to return to Harmony and brave the wrath of Emma's parents, in order to get some of her furniture and belongings. They went with apprehension, but they were welcomed by Isaac with open arms and an invitation to move back to Pennsylvania. Hale would provide them a place to live and help Joseph get into business. But events had already occurred which dictated that Joseph would not be a farmer.

On September 22, 1827, while they were in Manchester, Joseph brought home a bundle that he said contained some golden plates, on which were printed a revelation in ancient Egyptian. Joseph's mother reported the following account given by her son of the immediate events that led him to unearth the plates:

> While I was thus in the act of calling upon God, I discovered a light appearing in the room, which continued to increase until the room was lighter than at noonday, when immediately a personage appeared at my bedside, standing in the air, for his feet did not touch the floor. . . . He called me by name, and said unto me that he was a messenger sent from the presence of God to me, and that his name was Nephi, that God had a work for me to do. . . . He said there was a book deposited, written upon gold plates giving an account of the former inhabitants of this continent, and the source from whence they sprang. . . . Also, that there were two stones in silver bows, and these stones fastened to a breastplate, constituted what is called the Urim and Thummim, deposited with the plates; and the possession and use of these stones were what constituted seers in ancient or former times; and that God had prepared them for the purpose of translating the book.[22]

That night Joseph went to the place where the plates were buried, at what came to be called Hill Cumorah, dug them up and brought them home. They were to remain unseen to all but Joseph, though several years later several of his followers signed a statement swearing that Joseph showed them the plates. The bundle that he said contained the plates went with Joseph and Emma back to Harmony.

The Smiths made the four-day wagon journey to Harmony in December. They unloaded their goods, including the box of plates, into the little house on Isaac Hale's property. Joseph set to work almost immediately, not farming or hunting, but translating the golden plates.

Joseph would sit behind a curtain in their house dictating the translation, and the recorder would take down his words. His first recorder was Emma, although her brother would often help. Using the Urim and Thummim or another small stone placed in a hat, he would bury his face in the hat and dictate the revelation. The fruits of those first months of translation were to be lost, for a friend of Joseph's, Martin Harris, took the translation into his custody for safekeeping. His wife, Dolly, apparently jealous or skeptical regarding the secrecy surrounding the work, eventually stole and destroyed the manuscript. That part was not translated over again. Cynics point out that it might have then been possible to compare new translation with old. The opportunity never materialized, for Joseph received a revelation telling him to translate a different book that contained a history of the same events described in the lost translation. It was July, 1828. The new translation, with Martin Harris as scribe, began in the winter of 1828-29.

The revelation itself seemed to flow from Joseph. His ability to pour forth that constant stream of narrative and biblical quotation seemed in itself a testimony to its miraculous origins. The end result of all that labor, by Emma, Martin Harris, and others, came to be called the *Book of Mormon*. It is a combination of Bible passages, popular legend concerning the origin of the Indians in the lost tribes of Israel, speculation about the origin of what we now know to be Indian burial mounds, and imaginative piety, all cast in the forms of King James English. The latter touch gave the whole an aura of sanctity.[23] It was completed by July, 1829, in a burst of creative production. It was printed and put on sale in Palmyra at the end of March, 1830.

Several days later, on April 6, 1830, the Church of Christ, as it was at first called, was established with six members at Fayette, New York. Most of Smith's first converts came from South Bainbridge and Colesville, with a few from the Palmyra area. At that meeting, as they talked of who should be the head of the new church, Joseph reported to them a revelation in which he was named "Seer, a Translator, a Prophet, an Apostle of Jesus Christ, and Elder of the Church through the will of God the Father, and the grace of your Lord Jesus Christ."[24] This established him as the head of the Church, a position he would hold without successful challenge until his death. Joseph also revealed to them at that time many of the details concerning organization of the church. One of the first churches organized was at Colesville, where there were a number of converts centered around the family of Joseph Knight, Sr., the old family friend of the Smiths.

The existence of this new church swiftly generated opposition. It was of the nature of the religious revivals of the time to produce conflict. Conversion often conferred upon persons an overwhelming sense that they were right and others were wrong. Church divisions and dissention were common. The Mormons from the first occasioned an extraordinary amount of opposition, even for that time. In June, 1830, Joseph, Emma, and some others went to Colesville to baptize a number of people. On Saturday, a dam was built across a nearby stream to form a baptismal pool. During the night, a mob tore it down. On Monday morning, the members repaired the dam and thirteen persons, including Emma, were baptized. Hecklers shouted at them during the ceremony. Later, Joseph was meeting with the new members at the house of Newel Knight when a constable appeared to arrest Joseph on the charge of being a "disorderly person."[25] The constable, who became sympathetic to Joseph, took him through a jeering mob, whipping the horses to a gallop so that the new Prophet would not fall in the hands of a tar-and-feather party. They arrived in South Bainbridge where Joseph spent the night before his trial the next day. The trial on July 1, 1830 lasted all day. Joseph Knight hired two men knowledgeable in law, and many of his friends testified on his behalf. Joseph was acquitted. In the meantime Joseph Knight's property was raided and vandalized by his neighbors.

The acquittal was no sooner issued and Joseph Smith out the door than he was arrested again by another constable and taken to Broome County. His second trial was at Colesville, and the same two men defended him. After hours of argument and harangue, Joseph was finally acquitted again at four o'clock in the morning. Joseph and Emma left immediately for Harmony, in order to escape the mob. They remained there for a while, and even bought the property they were living on. Joseph was given a special revelation for Emma, naming her an "elect lady." Almost at once, he received another revelation to move his family to Waterloo. They left for Fayette, and Emma was never to see her family again. Isaac Hale had bitter words about his son-in-law the rest of his life.

The history of Joseph and the foundling church shifted from the upper Susquehanna to places further west—first to Kirtland, Ohio, and then to Nauvoo, Illinois. Joseph and his brother Hyrum were murdered by another mob at Carthage, near Nauvoo, in 1844. By then, the Church of Jesus Christ of the Latter Day Saints was much larger and stronger, though it continued to be surrounded by controversy. They found a measure of peace only when they moved into the wilderness of what was to become Utah.

There remained in Broome, Chenango, and Susquehanna Counties a body of legends and memories, some of which persist to this day. The one most often repeated is the walking-on-water story. Some put the event in Pennsylvania, others in New York. Apparently, at one time, there was a marker showing a purported place of the incident, near Ninevah, at the Broome-Chenango County line on the east side of the Susquehanna River. Bert Lord, a native of the area, wrote describing the incident in 1938:

> He had constructed planks which were just a few inches under the water where he was to do the walking; I assume feeling he would feel more secure with the planks under him than just treading the water. A great crowd assembled after evening fall and while he was demonstrating his walking on the water he got out some distance from the shore and suddenly went down all over. It seems some mischievous person had removed one of the

planks and altho Smith seemed to have all kinds of spiritual faith, when he came to where the plank was removed he went down.[26]

Another telling of the story had it happen once successfully. Joseph fell in on the second attempt when the plank was removed by "wicked boys."[27] A third account has the location at the Cornwall farm on the east side of the river at South Bainbridge. During haying, the Cornwalls discovered tracks going down to the river. Following them, they discovered a plank bridge just under the surface of the water extending to the other side. The boys then sawed mostly through one of the planks. That night when Joseph came with some of his converts, he started demonstrating his faith by walking on water. When he came to the weakened place, he fell through.[28]

There is little to indicate that the story in any of its versions is true. First of all it supposedly happened in 1827, well before he was involved with establishing a new religious movement. Second, the story has too much of the character of that brand of Yankee humor in which the know-it-all outsider is done in by the supposedly inferior locals. Third, all reporting of the story in print occurred long after Mormonism was established as a religious force to be reckoned with.

Another indication that legend frequently outstripped fact could be seen in a state historical marker, that at one time stood by a creek along Route 41 outside Afton, with the following inscription: "Joseph Smith in 1827 dug for and claimed to find some of the plates of the Mormon Bible, one-fourth mile up this creek."[29] That story probably arose out of the plethora of local accounts of Joseph searching for buried treasure, but it had no basis in fact or in Joseph's claims.

What is true is that the Church of Jesus Christ of the Latter Day Saints had its beginnings in the same religious enthusiasm that surrounded the growth of Methodism in New York and Northeastern Pennsylvania. One suspects that much of the opposition from Methodists and Presbyterians was due to the fact that the new religion drew many of its early converts from among the same people they sought to win to faith. The competition for the hearts of potential believers was harsh in that rough and tumble age. Out of that rugged time grew a strong Methodist Church. There also emerged the Mormons and their colorful founder, Joseph Smith. He was shaped by Yankee piety and Methodist camp meetings. In the unpredictable ways of history, his movement was set on its way by events and people in places that are very much a part of the history of the Wyoming Conference.

END NOTES

1. This point and many of the other points in this section are developed in detail in Whitney R. Cross, *The Burned-Over District: The Social and Intellectual History of Enthusiastic Religion in Western New York, 1800-1850* (New York: Harper & Row, Harper Torchbooks, 1965).

2. Cross, p. 11.

3. A. F. Chaffee, *History of the Wyoming Conference of the Methodist Episcopal Church* (New York: Eaton & Mains, 1904), p. 697.

4. Chaffee, p. 484.

5.   Quoted in Fawn M. Brodie, *No Man Knows My History: The Life of Joseph Smith* (New York: Alfred A. Knopf, 1972), Second Edition, p. 5. This is an excellent non-Mormon biography. An excellent Mormon biography is Donna Hill, *Joseph Smith, The First Mormon* (Garden City, New York: Doubleday & Company, 1977). A fine analysis of Mormon history, thought, and structure is Thomas F. O'Dea, *The Mormons* (Chicago: The University of Chicago Press, 1957).

6.   Lucy Smith, *Biographical Sketches of Joseph Smith the Prophet and His Progenitors for Many Generations* (Lamoni, Iowa: 1912). See, for example, pp. 53ff.

7.   Hill, p. 50.

8.   Hill, p. 52.

9.   Hill, pp. 52-53.

10.   Brodie, p. 20.

11.   Brodie, p. 20.

12.   Hill, p. 66.

13.   Chaffee, p. 45.

14.   Chaffee, p. 62.

15.   Rhamanthus M. Stocker, *Centennial History of Susquehanna County, Pennsylvania* (Philadelphia: 1887; Reprinted, Baltimore: Regional Publishing Co., 1974), pp. 544, 587.

16.   Quoted in Chaffee, p. 45.

17.   From Isaac Hale's testimony in the 1826 Bainbridge trial. Reprinted in Brodie, p. 439.

18.   James H. Smith, *History of Chenango and Madison Counties, New York* 1784-1880 (Syracuse, N. Y.: D. Mason & Co., 1880), p. 153.

19.   Account of the trial reprinted in Brodie, pp. 427-9. See also the analysis of the evidence in Wesley P. Walters, "Joseph Smith's Bainbridge, N. Y., Court Trials," *Westminister Theological Journal* 36 (Winter 1974): 123-155. Interpretations of the evidence are in Hill, pp. 65-66, and Brodie, pp. 30-31.

20.   Chaffee, pp. 162, 692; *Minutes*, Wyoming Annual Conference, Methodist Episcopal Church, 1872, p. 34.

21.   Brodie, p. 32; Hill, p. 69.

22.   Lucy Smith, *Sketches*, pp. 83-86. *The Doctrine and Covenants* of the LDS Church records the revealing angel to be Moroni, not Nephi. Section 2.

23.   For a more detailed account of contents and sources that Joseph may have drawn from for the *Book of Mormon*, see Brodie, pp. 57-66; O'Dea, pp. 22ff; Hill, pp. 98ff.

24.   *Doctrine and Covenants* 21.1-5.

25.   Walters, p. 124.

26.   Quoted in an unpublished manuscript by Charles Decker, a local historian who presently lives in Afton, New York.

27.   Smith, *Chenango and Madison Counties*, p. 154.

28.   Oneonta *Herald*, January 18, 1900.

29.   Decker MS.

FROM TRAVELING PREACHER TO SETTLED PASTOR:
CHANGES IN THE ITINERANT MINISTRY

Keith Beasley-Topliffe

On September 30, 1785, John Wesley wrote to Francis Asbury concerning the length of appointments:

> I myself may perhaps have as much variety of matter as many of our preachers. Yet I am well assured, were I to preach three years together in one place, both the people and myself would grow as dead as stones. Indeed, this is quite contrary to the whole economy of Methodism; God has always wrought among us by a constant change of preachers.[1]

A century later, Wesley's remarks had become the great prooftext in the defense of the rapidly turning wheels of the itineracy—the "constant change of preachers" from place to place.

Now, another century later, when the discussion turns to length of pastoral appointments, it is much more likely to revolve around studies by Lyle Schaller:

> . . . From the congregation's perspective the most effective years of a pastorate rarely begin before the fourth or fifth or sixth or seventh, and sometimes even the eighth, year of that pastorate. . . . What does this pattern say to the question, Has the time come for me to move? . . . If that question is being asked in the third year, the response may be, Don't move, your best years here have yet to begin![2]

Could any two statements be further apart? And yet the key to their difference comes in just two words. Wesley spoke of the stationing of "preachers." Schaller speaks of a "pastorate." As Methodism has grown from a frontier evangelistic movement into a large denomination in settled towns and cities, its ministers have changed from traveling preachers—the circuit riders—to settled pastors. This change was a hard one, strongly resisted by many, and still not peacefully finished.

The great circuits were already disappearing when our Conference was formed, in 1852. Forty-two years earlier, the Tioga Circuit had required several weeks and over four hundred miles of travel to reach all thirty of its preaching places. It stretched from Wyalusing to Caroline, and from Elmira to Binghamton. But in 1812, the formation of the Broome Circuit took away a hundred miles and ten stops. After 1828 it was broken into a number of smaller pieces.

Even in those early days, not all circuits were so huge. George Peck, who started his ministry with the two hundred miles and twenty-eight stations of the Broome Circuit, looked back fondly at his third appointment: "In 1818 Wyoming Circuit embraced what is now divided between eighteen pastoral charges, and then it had the reputation of being a comfortable little circuit, nearly as easy as a station."[3]

As the area became more settled, the size of the circuits decreased steadily—apparently to keep the membership of each appointment under five hundred or so. In 1850, the Lanesboro Circuit still had twenty points, but it only covered an area about thirty miles long and fifteen wide. Just a year later it was divided into three parts, which, within a few years, had been subdivided still further.

By the time our Conference was formed, then, most of the appointments were small enough for the preacher to spend his nights at home, and ride out during the day. Several of the city churches were on their own as stations. Yet, for all that the situation was changing radically, the Methodist preachers still thought of themselves as traveling preachers, out to win the world for Christ. And, while some of their success may be put down to the population growth in the area, much of the credit goes to a sense of purpose and a system uniquely suited to rapid evangelism.

The purpose was stated simply in the minutes of the "Christmas Conference" of 1784:

> Question 4. What may we reasonably believe to be God's Design in raising up the Preachers called Methodists?
>
> Answer. To reform the Continent, and to spread scriptural Holiness over these Lands.[4]

The Pastoral Address at the first session of our Conference repeated this call to arms:

> There is a vast field before us "white unto the harvest." . . . Our faith and our zeal for the cause of God, and the salvation of souls, must pause at no barriers. National and denominational prejudices must not be regarded as insuperable obstacles in the way of preaching Christ crucified, in any locality where souls are perishing for lack of knowledge. Influenced by these convictions we enter the field assigned us, with a firm purpose to preach the gospel to all within our reach. . . .[5]

The preachers were the soldiers in this evangelistic warfare, under the command of the superintendency. But what was the role of the laypeople? Their job was to support the preachers in their work, to "furnish the means of subsistence."

> Your liberality must meet our necessities: your presence must stay our hands; and your prayers must come up before God continually that He may send down his blessings upon our united efforts, and command the desired increase.[6]

Disunity in the churches, or even "the least alienation of affection" from the preacher, was regarded as treason against this all-important mission, and so "an evil of fearful magnitude." Let those who wanted to relax go elsewhere.

> Methodism is essentially aggressive—its propagandism is necessary to its very being—and wherever its true spirit imbues the souls of the whole mass . . . a man might as well attempt to roll back the swelling tide of old ocean, or to chain the lightning as to stop its onward progress.[7]

In the early days of American Methodism, the circuit rider was the force that so caused the tide to swell and the lightning to flash. While other denominations carefully trained clergy and established mission churches, the traveling preachers charged into every corner of the young nation, gathering a group wherever possible. Buildings were no concern, for the Methodists met in barns, schoolhouses, private homes. In 1816, the Broome Circuit included no churches in its twenty-eight stops. The twenty stops on the 1850 Lanesboro circuit included only three churches, two of them less than two years old. The willingness of the circuit riders to go any place, any time led to the saying, "It's weather fit only for crows and Methodist preachers."

The use of military metaphors for the circuit riders was thoroughly apt. They had little choice of assignment. They were sent—deployed—by the bishop, and moved often to new assignments. The General Conference of 1804 set the maximum stay at two years, but changes were more often yearly, and sometimes even more frequent. The life was hard—and only the strong survived. The rest choose to settle down as local preachers, or died young. Marriage was actively discouraged, and often punished with forcible location.

And yet the system worked, better than any other, at least as far as accomplishing its purpose of reforming the continent. There were at least two primary reasons for this success. The first is that it made the most of limited numbers. In 1784 there were only 83 traveling preachers for the whole nation.[8] The large circuits allowed these men to have some influence over a great number of members, spread over a wide area. The system was, as George Peck put it, "a labourer-saving" device.

> The pastoral service, which otherwise would have been confined to a single parish, is extended by this plan to scores, and sometimes hundreds, of towns and villages, and, by the co-operation of the class meeting, is rendered almost as efficient as it would be were it local.[9]

The class meeting was indeed a vital part of the plan, for it was there that the real pastoral work was done. The circuit rider might visit a preaching stop less than twelve times before moving to a new circuit. But the class leader was there all the time, and knew the lives of his or her group. This "local pastoring" was also supported by the exhorter, a beginning preacher whose task was to bring the circuit rider's general message home to local problems. Proven exhorters might go on to become local preachers, and could be ordained in that capacity. The class leaders, exhorters, and local preachers—all serving without any pay—enabled the circuit riders to ride on, confident that the fruits of their labors would be preserved.

The second advantage of the circuit rider system was that it made the most of limited education or limited abilities. The circuit riders were not carefully trained seminary graduates. Few had more than an elementary education. They reached their responsibilities by a careful series of steps, rising through the ranks of Methodism.

The first several steps were mentioned above: member, class leader, exhorter, local preacher. Here, again, the class meeting was an indispensible part of the system. In the classes, members began to learn how to talk about their Christian experience and how to help others express their faith. Part of the class leader's job was to spot talent, and nurture any new-born sense of call to preach.

Someone who had progressed to local preacher could be admitted on trial as a traveling preacher. Two years later he could become a traveling deacon, and traveling elder in another two. There were no educational requirements, for it was experience and talent that really mattered. Anyone surviving to this stage had passed through trial by fire.

This is not to say that the preachers were ignorant. They picked up their education on the road. Preachers were urged to spend from six to twelve every morning in prayerful study, in addition to an hour of prayer and scripture reading on rising and before bedtime. Many of the preachers read copiously, and some even taught themselves Greek, Latin, or Hebrew. The General Conference of 1816 urged each annual conference to create a course of study for preachers, and in 1848 the reading list was standardized for the whole Methodist Episcopal Church.

To the reading programs should be added the benefits of varied experience. At least, the preachers themselves made much of the "school of hard knocks." Here is George Peck again:

> Circumstances furnish the most effectual education to men. No man, above fatuity, could occupy the large spheres of our fathers, without a correspondent enlargement of soul. Our old circuits were the best means ever devised for the development of every energetic quality, and the acquisition of every practical qualification which could be acquired out of the study.[10]

In a later writing, though, Peck admitted that the long rides on horseback might have quite the opposite effect: "a tendency to mental inactivity, and a temptation to substitute physical for mental effort."[11]

But while the system produced proven, dedicated preachers, it did not ensure that they had a lot to say. Rather, it saved them from having to worry about much variety. George Peck put it somewhat more bluntly: "Small abilities went much further than they can with our present system."[12] Twelve sermons, repeated twenty to thirty times each year, might suffice. And after a few years, those sermons would be highly polished gems. The constant moves meant that the preachers could repeat their sermons—but also that the people would hear a fresh batch every year. Over several years, they would be treated to a wide variety of styles and emphases.

It is no wonder, then, that the prospect of smaller circuits or even stations looked frightening to many of the circuit riders. Preaching to the same congregation, perhaps as often as three times a week, meant up to one hundred fifty sermons in a year! Many of the preachers (remember Wesley's letter to Asbury!) doubted they had that much to say—a doubt firmly shared by their people.

But there was no stopping the settling of America. As the membership in the Methodist Church grew, the circuits had to get smaller. More city churches became stations. While clergy of the less settled South and West protested this "cutting up the work," their Northeastern brothers explained that the same would happen when their population grew, and they, too, would petition for the division of annual conferences. During the debate on the division of the Genessee Conference (to form the Wyoming Conference)

George Peck made his first speech to General Conference. He recalls the reaction:

> One of the fathers sarcastically said that he had heard of a circuit in New England that had "six rest days in a week." This story amused many of the members, and raised quite a laugh at the expense of the Genessee boys. We, however, held on to our purpose. . . . This work of cutting up conferences, districts, and circuits has been going on from that day to this; and nothing has more clearly indicated the growth of Methodism in the country than this same process of "cutting up the work."[13]

The itinerant system had covered deficiencies that could be easily overlooked in evangelistic pioneers. The lack of formal education was no great barrier to the circuit rider, moved frequently. After all, the Methodists were the only religious groups in some areas, so the choice had been Methodism or nothing. But now, particularly in the cities, the Methodists were in competition with other, better educated clergy. George Peck was alarmed at the prospect.

> But now we fix untrained men in small stations, amid the closest competition, where they are overburdened with pastoral duties, which were unknown to our fathers, and expect them to maintain our cause with success among a population the most enlightened on the globe. How is it possible for a young man, without discipline, without a knowledge of books or of men, to furnish instruction for one or two years, under such circumstances? A few of our most vigorous minds may nerve themselves for the necessities of such a position, but our aggregate ministry must necessarily fall into the rear of the educated ministers of other sects.[14]

The Church was reluctant to adapt to the new situation. Some, like Peck, called for more education for the preachers. At about the time Peck was writing the above, the first Methodist seminaries were founded, under the code name of "Biblical Institutes." The course of study was standardized and strengthened. Methodist preachers—or at least some of them—were able to "maintain the cause with success" even in the cities.

But other voices called against all this educational hoopla as a danger to the spirit of Methodism and an invitation to heresy. The secret of Methodism's success had always been the itineracy. Surely it held the secret in this new situation as well. It was no longer so useful as a "laborer-saving device," nor could it compensate for a general lack of education. But now, two different areas were held up as strengths of the system.

The first was that it still was a test of stamina and sincerity. The rapid change of circuits could be likened to panning for gold. As the water swirled about in the pan, the light dirt flew out, and only the gold was left in the bottom. So those who were weak, or over-much interested in material wealth or a stable life, would soon drop out or migrate to other denominations. Only true Methodists would survive the system. "Place hunters," explained Charles Crane, "naturally gravitate to other denominations where easy and luxurious settled pastorates are found. A preacher who doesn't want to be on the march falls out and settles."[15]

But the greatest—or at least most common—argument in favor of a rapid change of pastorates was that it allowed the preachers to specialize.

There was no need to produce well-rounded clergy. Over the course of ten years, a charge would see (before 1864, at least) a minimum of five different pastors. If the bishop was doing his job, these folks should among them cover all the needs of the charge. The argument was quite thoroughly stated by Abel Stevens.

> Many men of fervid spirit and deep piety have little talent for disciplining the Church. Their discourses are chiefly hortative; they are instrumental in great revivals and additions to the membership. It is obvious that such talents need a rapid distribution. . . . By an itinerant system such men are changed from position to position, arousing dull Churches, breaking up new ground, invading and reclaiming ungodly neighborhoods. By the same system prudent men, with talents for instructing and edifying the converted masses, follow the former, gathering up and securing the fruits of their labors. Some pastors are addicted chiefly to experimental and practical preaching, others to the illustration and defense of doctrinal truth. Some are more effectual in social services, others in the ministration of the pulpit. Some have ability only for spiritual labors; others are skillful in managing and invigorating the fiscal resources of the Church, in erecting new chapels, and promoting the benevolent enterprises of the times.[16]

The argument seemed persuasive. What other system could bring such a wide range of talents to every situation? And yet, between the lines lies the fundamental change which has brought longer and longer appointments to our Church. Look again at the skills being described. Alongside preaching, the nurture and instruction of new members and involvement in social services have appeared. These are pastoral functions. They were tasks unknown to the circuit riders. Nurture, in fact, was the purpose of the class meeting. But when the preacher was settled in the midst of his people, the class leader began to seem less useful. There were attempts to revitalize the class by changing it into an educational session, but by the 1850's the classes were dying. The southern Methodists made class membership optional in 1866, followed shortly by the northern Church. But this action was really only acknowledging what had already happened. The preacher had become the pastor.

A preacher can preach anywhere, any time. It is helpful to be acquainted with one's audience, but not absoultely necessary. It is much more difficult to be a "walk-in" pastor. It takes time to build trust, to understand what is happening, to get to know the people. And so it was only natural that the change from preacher to pastor would be accompanied by a call for longer appointments, particularly in the stations.

The first change was small. In 1864, the General Conference raised the time limit from two to three years. Our Conference was quick to take advantage of the change. Of 128 appointments in effect in 1865, 44—more than a third—lasted for three years.[17] Soon people were calling for another increase in the time limit.

Somehow, though, this battle became symbolic of the changes going on in Methodism. The circuits were cut up, the classes disappearing. If the preachers stopped moving, what would be left of the glorious past? Nor was it our past alone. In 1884, Bishop Henry Warren offered our Annual Conference an earlier model: "Paul has been called the Methodist apostle. He was an itinerant of itinerants, seldom staying in the same place more than three years unless he was in prison."[18] What Bishop Warren failed to mention was that Paul was a preacher, not a pastor.

There were two dangers frequently mentioned in debate about the time limit: heresy and congregationalism (which, after all, was organizational heresy to many Methodists). There was concern that a long pastorate could become ingrown, and so corrupt an entire congregation. This was the decisive point for one writer:

> But it is as the bulwark of sound doctrine that the itineracy commends itself to every sincere believer in the doctrines and lover of the spirit of Methodism. . . . The preacher of false doctrines remains at the longest but three years the pastor of one congregation. It is impossible for him to eradicate in so short a time the seeds of truth planted by his predecessors. And on his departure a man both sound in doctrine and able to defend and establish the truth may be appointed to fill his place.[19]

Why did Buckley think a bishop would allow such a pastor to remain in place even three years? The question brings us to the second fear: congregationalism. Many writers assumed that if there were no time limit on appointments, Methodism would quickly "degenerate" into a call system. The time limit removed responsibility from Bishop, preacher, and church for forforcing a move. Without this external pressure, though, would it be possible to pry pastors out of the choicest pulpits? Or, for that matter, would the worst places ever be able to rid themselves of the worst preachers?

The call to extend the time limit came before the Annual Conference in 1884, and was firmly rejected:

> Resolved. That in the judgment of this Conference the time limit in our itineracy is a necessity. (2) That the time for extending the limit beyond three years has not come.[20]

The Lay Electoral Convention meeting at the same time (laity were elected to attend General Conference after 1868, but were not part of the Annual Conference until 1932) adopted even stronger language:

> . . . It is the firm conviction of the members of this convention that the rule of itineracy should not be in the least abated or abandoned, and . . . the time for remaining as preacher in charge of one society should not be increased beyond three years.[21]

Such sentiments won the day in 1884, but four years later the issue was raised again. The laity repeated their objections, but the clergy changed their tune. After long debate and a display of parliamentary maneuvering, they voted (85-62) to "respecfully memorialize the approaching General Conference" to extend the limit to four years.[22]

When the General Conference extended the limit to five years, our Conference, however reluctant to see the change, was again quick to take advantage of it. Of 190 appointments which included 1889, 27 lasted the full five years, and another 32 for four—accounting for thirty per cent of the appointments. Another 57 lasted three years. One of the four year appointments was that of A. F. Brown, author of the 1884 resolution.

Had this extension of the time weakened the bishop's authority? The question was soon tested when, in 1892, Lyman Weeks refused his appointment to LeRaysville. This did not mean that he kept his old appointment, though. He sat out the year. At the next session of the Annual Conference, a committee investigated the case and decided "that satisfactory acknowledgment of error had been made. . . . There were extenuating circumstances and the offender had much sympathy throughout the conference on account of his good work and splendid record in other years."[23]

Things were changing, though. The "consultative process," though by no means mandated or even suggested in the *Discipline,* had been born. One example from 1894 seems to be coming close to the fears of a call system. It was reported as a sidebar to the account of the Conference meetings.

> Rev. J. B. Sweet, of Ashley, is so much in favor with his people that when they heard the Norwich, N. Y., people were after him they sent a committee post haste to the bishop with an emphatic protest. The bishop thought he ought to send Mr. Sweet to Norwich, as it was a hearty call and an advance for this popular young clergyman. But he left the matter with Mr. Sweet himself, and he, at the solicitation of his people, agreed to remain. The Ashley people ought now to treat Mr. Sweet as fairly as he has treated them, and give him a substantial increase of salary.[24]

John Sweet stayed in Ashley for four years (two more), and then went on to Simpson in Scranton for a five year stay.

If the increase to five years worked so well, why not remove the limit entirely? Most of the churches were not affected by the time limit, since less than fifteen per cent of the appointments lasted five years. Why not seek the benefit of those churches which could make use of longer pastorates? The need was especially felt in the cities, where a long stay would give the Methodist pastor a chance to become well-known, and therefore influential, in the community. A District Superintendent from California asked, "What would the commercial world think of removing clerks as soon as they become thoroughly familiar with their trade and customers; . . . or of a government that denied congressmen and senators the privilege of re-election?"[25]

The idea was rejected in 1896, but came up again in 1900. The Wyoming Conference suggested an alternative to a complete removal of the limit. The plan allowed a Quarterly Conference to petition the bishop, on the vote, without debate, of three-quarters of those present, for a renewal of appointment for a sixth, seventh, eighth, ninth, or tenth year. Ten years remained as an absolute limit. This idea was passed unanimously by the Annual Conference.[26] The General Conference, however, opted for simplicity. The time limit was completely removed for all pastors.

Once again, the churches and Cabinet of our Conference took advantage of the new rules. Of 212 appointments made or renewed in 1901, 27 lasted more than five years, the longest being C. E. Mogg's sixteen years at Central, Wilkes-Barre. Another 58 appointments lasted either four or five years. These numbers have continued to grow ever since. Of 184 appointments made or renewed in 1976, 88 lasted six or more years (33 of them at least ten years). Twenty-seven of these are still in effect. Another 52 lasted four or five years, and only 44 stopped before that. The average appointment lasted over six years.

The giant circuits are gone. The class meeting is ancient history. The time limit has disappeared. In 1843, George Peck reflected the assumptions of the day when he warned, "The time when the itineracy shall cease in our ministry and classes among our laity will be the date of our downfall."[27] It wasn't, though. Rather, it was the time when our traveling preachers became settled pastors, when the system changed, however reluctantly, to meet a changed society.

The United Methodist Church continues, and so does the itineracy. The power of the bishop to make appointments was recently tested again in our Conference, and confirmed upon appeal to the Judicial Council. The idea of consultation is now part of the *Discipline,* but has not turned us into a congregational church with a call system. If we can conclude anything from this history, it is that the strength of our Church has never been in a particular system, but in its ability to adapt the system to the needs of the society in which the Church exists. May God grant us the courage to continue seek the best possible means to fulfill the task set before us two centuries ago: "to reform the Continent, and to spread scriptural Holiness over these Lands."

END NOTES

1. Letter of 30 September 1785, quoted by O. H. Warren in "The Time Restriction in the Methodist Itineracy," *Methodist Review, Vol. 70,* (March, 1888), p. 234.

2. Lyle E. Schaller, *Survival Tactics in the Parish* (Nashville: Abingdon, 1977), p. 27.

3. George Peck, *The Past and the Present. A Semi-Centennial Sermon* (New York: Carlton and Porter, 1866), p. 20. This was a sermon preached to the Wyoming Conference on the fiftieth anniversary of Peck's first appointment as traveling preacher.

4. Quoted by Don W. Holter in "Some Changes Related to the Ordained Ministry in the History of American Methodism," *Methodist History, Vol. xiii, No. 3* (April 1975), p. 179.

5. *Minutes of the Wyoming Annual Conference, 1852,* p. 27.

6. *Ibid.,* p. 28.

7. *Ibid.,* p. 28.

8. Holter, p. 182.

9. George Peck, *Sketches and Incidents; or, A Budget from the Saddle-bags of a Superannuated Itinerant* (New York: Carlton and Porter, 1843), p. 126f. This was published anonymously. Peck is identified as the author in the catalog of the United Methodist Archives at Drew University. He was *not* "superannuated" at that time, nor for thirty years after.

10. George Peck, *Sketches from the Study of a Superannuated Itinerant* (Boston: Charles H. Pierce and Co., 1851), p. 207. Also published anonymously as above.

11. Peck, 1866, p. 30.

12. Peck, 1851, p. 208.

13. Peck, 1866, p. 40.

14. Peck, 1851, p. 208f.

15. Charles A. Crane, *The Itinerant Preacher,* p. 11. This is a sermon preached to the New England Conference on 13 April 1899. Published as a pamphlet.

16. Quoted by J. M. Buckley in "The Itinerant Ministry of the Methodist Episcopal Church," *Methodist Quarterly Review* (January, 1880), p. 141.

17. These and other statistics are based on lists of appointments in *History of the Wyoming Conference of the Methodist Episcopal Church,* by A. F. Chaffee (New York: Eaton and Mains, 1904); in the "Historical Record (Fifty Years) of Churches and their Pastors" mimeographed as a supplement to the 1962 *Year Book* of the Wyoming Conference; and in recent copies of the *Journal* of the Wyoming Conference. They are as accurate as possible, but not necessarily exhaustive.

18. Sermon by Bishop Henry W. Warren, quoted in *Scranton Republican* March 31, 1884.

19. Buckley, p. 143.

20. *Scranton Republican,* March 31, 1884.

21. *Scranton Republican,* March 29, 1884.

22. *Minutes of the Wyoming Annual Conference, 1888,* p. 51.

23. *Scranton Republican,* April 15, 1893.

24. *Scranton Republican,* April 17, 1894.

25. E. W. Caswell, *Shall the Time Limit Be Removed by the General Conference of 1896* (No publisher listed), p. 22.

26. *Minutes of the Wyoming Annual Conference, 1900,* p. 49f.

27. Peck, 1843, p. 127.

THE AUTHORITY OF THE CONFERENCE

William B. Lawrence

One autumn day, as a United Methodist minister was opening his mail, he noticed in the envelope from the Wyoming Conference office an appeal from one of the Conference institutions. The Children's Home was soliciting labels from Campbell soup products: the Home, in turn, could redeem the labels for recreation equipment which would be used in its program; church groups were being invited to help the Home by collecting and sending quantities of labels.

Further down in the minister's mail pile was his September issue of *The Interpreter,* the only publication in wide general circulation among ministers and members of United Methodist Churches today. Leafing through the magazine, he noticed an article about Campbell's soup products—and why United Methodists should boycott them.[1] Specifically, the article urged members of the denomination not to participate in the label redemption program.

The dilemma in which the minister found himself would have been amusing, were it not so agonizing. Should his congregation support the work of an Annual Conference institution, to improve recreation for children, by buying Campbell's soup and saving the labels? Or should the efforts of a General Conference board to secure justice for tomato growers be supported by boycotting Campbell products? Should his congregation see the company as the benefactor, or as the enemy of the United Methodist mission?

What should he do?

There was a time in Methodist history when it was very clear where—and to whom—a preacher should go for an answer to that question. John Wesley's "conferences" with his preachers began in 1744 by addressing three questions:

1. What to teach;
2. How to teach; and
3. What to do.[2]

Preachers took their troubles to Wesley who, in conference with his preachers, told them what to do. Until his death in 1791, there is no doubt that John Wesley was the authority for all Methodist decisions and courses of action.

In modern Methodism, there is no such clear center of authority. As a result, the Campbell soup episode becomes something other than an isolated case. An annoying uncertainty pervades many hard choices. Occasionally an ennervating drama unfolds, such as the case of Eddie James Carthan, mayor of a small Mississippi town, who was arrested and jailed on a number of serious charges including assault and homicide. His detractors had long considered him to be a threat to the community and a destructive force: the murder charge merely confirmed their worst suspicions. His supporters considered those suspicions to be thinly disguised racism: the murder charge merely confirmed their view that Mr. Carthan, who is black, was cruelly victimized and framed by his opponents. United Methodists were polarized by the case: funds from the denomination flowed in to provide for his legal defense, out of concern for justice to be done toward him; congregations, and their annual conference and episcopal leadership in the area, rebelled at this intrusion without consulting United Methodists in the region.

Thus the question—"What to do?" Where, and with whom, does the authority to decide lie?

I

Church bodies and Christian denominations locate their centers of authority differently. In the Roman Catholic Church, for instance, Vatican II settled the issue: authority resides in the office of Bishop, pre-eminently in the Bishop of Rome.[3] An Ecumenical Council, consisting of all Bishops, writes the Constitutions for the Church. A College of Bishops drafts its positions on such issues as nuclear weapons and interfaith marriages (though it has no authority apart from the Pope). A priest is defined as a "Bishop's assistant."[4] And the role of the laity is of a separate order, non-hierarchical and non-authoritative. Should a priest or parishioner face a dilemma and wonder what to do about boycotts or defense funds, the Roman Catholic Church understands that the Bishop will decide.

Among Baptists, authority resides elsewhere; but its location is just as clear. The congregation decides. When a Baptist Convention or Mission Board acts, the congregation has authority to affirm or reject the action. Decisions about fitness for membership and pastoral leadership are made by the congregation. A preacher is amenable solely to his or her members, not to a higher judicatory.

However, United Methodists have no single clear authority center. According to Paul McCleary of the denomination's Structure Study Commission in 1971, four authority centers function in the denomination: the episcopacy, the conference, the judiciary, and the general boards.[5]

One might be tempted to argue that, in broad perspective, there has been very nearly a chronological progression of relative importance from one authority center to the next. Francis Asbury's rather authoritarian approach to the *episcopacy* dominated the early days of American Methodism.[6] He was its "almost unchallenged leader;" and, when challenged, his word was generally affirmed as authoritative. One such challenge, though it did not necessarily diminish his own authoritative position, arose in opposition to Asbury's plan for a council to manage American Methodism. It would have "perserved his power in all affairs of the church" according to Frederick

Norwood.[8] But the plan failed, and that led a reluctant Asbury to support the concept of a General Conference beginning in 1792.

Of course, the "Conference" had been at the heart of Methodism since the first session back in 1744. Yet Wesley was clearly the authority who dominated each conference. The 1784 Christmas Conference in Baltimore, which is the occasion for claiming a Methodist bicentennial in 1984, was also conducted under the aegis of Wesley, through his appointed superintendents Coke and Asbury. Asbury, of course, emerged as the authority: for instance, when Richard Whatcoat was elevated to the episcopacy, it was as an auxiliary to Asbury.

A year after Wesley's death, however, the *Conference* exerted its own authority. It disposed of Asbury's plan for a council. It demanded that quadrennial sessions be held.[9] It developed, in 1796, its own plan to recruit and evaluate ministerial candidates.[10] As a General Conference, it assumed authority over the annual conferences.[11]

Meanwhile, it became clear that American Methodism was not going to operate exclusively either under the hand of an episcopal authority or by the votes of succeeding conferences. A Methodist constitution was adopted in 1808, and thus the *judiciary* came into prominence as a center of authority—for someone had to determine which actions were or were not constitutional. The Conference, to be sure, functioned in this capacity itself, but not without difficulty. As early as the first General Conference in 1792, James O'Kelly had sought a process by which a minister could appeal an appointment "if anyone thinks himself injured by the appointment."[12] Though the motion failed, the need for some grievance procedure became apparent, especially with the waning of Asbury's individual authority and the acceptance of episcopal fallibility. In later years the judicial center became an important channel for lay appeal and lay oversight of church decisions.

Along the way, *program bodies*—the ancestors of today's general boards—were becoming centers of authority. The Methodist Book Concern was the first of them, but publication efforts expanded into the agencies which directed the growing mission and benevolence causes of the late 19th and early 20th centuries.[13] Funds today are allocated and personnel are chosen according to a mechanism which operates essentially by its own authority, subject to the quadrennially defined budgets and policies of the General Conference.

Thus, several interlocking (and often competing) authority centers function in the United Methodist system, having emerged in our history. This balance of authority has probably helped ameliorate the tension apparent in Methodism between authoritarian and democratic impulses.[14] It has, nevertheless, been further confused by another important authority center in the practical life of the United Methodist Church—the congregation. James O'Kelly's request for an appeal to an injurious appointment has never been formally accepted by the denomination, but now an elaborate consultative process is required prior to decisions about ministerial assignments. Congregations have continued to exercise some exclusive authority, notably in the area of Christian education: for years, as the Journals of the Wyoming

Conference reveal,[15] there has been less than whole-hearted acceptance of the denominational curriculum materials. Local churches have found ways to accrue to themselves the mark of authority.

To cloud the issue even further, an anti-authority mystique has taken hold in the religious culture surrounding 20th century American Methodism. Catholic laity no longer accede to their Bishop's pronouncements on contraception; nor have episcopal efforts prevented Catholic women from seeking abortions at a rate about equal to their percentage of the total population.[16] Baptists have found it possible to choose racial justice as a principle of authority higher than the priority of the congregation—witness the schism among Baptists in Plains, Georgia, in the late 1970's. Russian Orthodox laity have taken their Bishops and priests into civil court litigation over the change of date for celebrating Christmas.

It is a phenomenon which clearly impinges upon the sense of authority among Wesley's ecclesiastical heirs. The Eddie Carthan and Campbell's soup cases in point are but two instances where one center of authority or another has been renounced—a program board overrode local congregations, an annual conference, and a bishop in the Carthan matter; an annual conference institution and a program board operated with independent authority in the Campbell case. But there have been others. The authority of a general board to conduct its global mission enterprise in its chosen way has been challenged by the Good News Movement. The authority of a bishop to appoint a minister to a congregation has been met by a physical barrier to the pulpit in one Connecticut church and by thunderous chords from the organ when the appointee's name was announced;[17] in another, the bishop's appointee was locked out of the church building and the Wyoming Conference took the Glenwood United Methodist Church to court.[18]

So the anti-authority phenomenon has clearly impinged upon the sense of authority among John Wesley's successors. "What to do?"

II

In the days when Wesley was the authority without peer, settling doctrinal matters, appointing preachers, determining conference dates and agenda, deciding whom to invite as conferees—all were within his own prerogative. Even in America, after the Revolution, when Asbury tried to remove the name of the "Founder" from disciplinary authority in 1787, he was overruled.[19] Such authority centers as emerged after his passing—notably the judiciary and program boards—and the struggles between the episcopacy and the conference for dominance were details he could not have envisioned.

However, he apparently had envisioned the situation after his passing clearly enough to believe that one authority center would be desirable. And he said that the *Conference* should be the authority.[20] Despite his dominance of it, the Conference had acquired an institutional character: he saw it not as a meeting of preachers but as that body of persons who gathered to confer.[21] Albert Outler says that the Conference "was one of those strokes of practical genius that marked" the Methodist movement.[22] Only because of the Conference, perhaps, did Wesley's movement remain crystalized and survive him.

When the Christmas Conference was being planned 200 years ago, the memories and documents of Wesley's early Conferences were at hand.[23] Forty years earlier, at the first Conference, three questions were addressed: What to teach, how to teach, what to do. Clearly the Conference had the authority to answer. The relative impact of personalities and problems introduced shifts in the Conference's embrace of its authority. But the design of the Founder and the direction of his movement's early history strongly suggested that the Conference remain pre-eminent in authority.

Historical and practical necessity split the Conference into General and Annual components. But two dramatic incidents recently have served to enhance the relative position of one over the other. The Carthan case, for example, was resolved by a Judicial Council decision that the program board overstepped its authority, by intruding its staff and resources into Mississippi, without prior request by the Annual Conference leadership or its Bishop. In the Roman Catholic hierarchy, the Pope can intrude directly at any time into the affairs of a diocese, but in the United Methodist system, an agency of the General Conference cannot, on its own initiative, intrude uninvited into an Annual Conference.

A second case involved the matter of homosexuals who seek ordination and election to Conference membership as United Methodist ministers. The long and troublesome debate over homosexuality within the denomination is not so germane here as the decision to uphold the clear position of the *Book of Discipline*—that Annual Conferences have exclusive control over whom to elect to membership and ordination, within the procedures and guidelines established by the *Discipline*.

Thus, in two celebrated issues, other authorities defer to the authority of the Annual Conference which now, in crises like the Carthan matter or the Campbell's soup troubles or the question of homosexuals in ministry, must decide "what to do?"

And that is precisely the question which the Conference is ill-prepared to face, in significant part because for most of its two centuries, that is the major question into which Methodists have generally transmuted their problems. Dilemmas have been addressed in terms of what can be "done" to manage the difficulty—in other words, as matters of polity or administration rather than theology. We have leaped to the question "What to do?" We have short-circuited the doctrinal concerns about "What to teach?" and "How to teach?" and we have done it for most of the bicentennial years that we now commemorate. In the early years of American Methodism, Conferences assumed that theological concerns had been sufficiently handled by Wesley himself. The Conference treated his *Notes, Sermons, Minutes,* and "Articles" as something akin to a closed canon.[24] What had happened in Conference with regard to teaching (and what he presumably wanted the Conference to do) was neglected. His doctrines were deemed acceptable even if his instruments for management were in need of amending. Methodists became practiced at polity while they atrophied in matters of doctrine. Conferences found ways to construe theological issues as polity decisions.[25]

In 1842, for instance, the General Conference was entrapped by what it saw as a polity question—"what to do" about slavery. Its handling, or mishandling, of the issue occasioned schism that brought into being the Wesleyan Methodist Church. What the Conference managed not to see was the theological issue at hand—"what to teach" about the doctrine of sanctification.[26] That, of course, was at the very heart of John Wesley's theological argument. Scriptural holiness, the goal of being made perfect in love in this life, could not be made compatible with slavery. But the theological point was lost upon the Conference, and the Wesleyans left.

A concern for doctrine, even at the Annual Conference level, was not entirely absent, to be sure. In 1852, at the first session of the Wyoming Annual Conference in Carbondale, Pennsylvania, there was a heresy trial. Cassius H. Harvey of Kingston and Charles Perkins were accused of abetting the doctrines of Spiritualism and were directed to recant: Harvey refused and was suspended from the Methodist Episcopal Church; Perkins recanted and was allowed to stay.[27]

But even that trial was less a theological debate than an administrative procedure. The offender was held up to objective standards, and the remedy was either to secure the offender's cessation of propogating the Spiritualistic doctrine or to dismiss him. It seems to have been handled as a scandal rather than a seminar, in a way not very different from James O'Kelly's departure a half century before.

When the Wyoming Conference attended to doctrine, it did so only in passing. There was, for instance, the golden anniversary Conference session in 1902, when the poet laureate of the era, a preacher named Charles L. Rice, read a composition for the occasion. Shortly afterward, he died, and he was eulogized as "thoroughly Methodistic, loving our doctrines and disciplines as well, and in his departure one of the links is broken that bound the early to the modern."[28]

Perhaps the closest that the Wyoming Conference came to formal theological conversation occurred at the time would-be preachers were examined in their fitness to continue in the course of study or to go into membership on trial. Each year the Conference Journal published the schedule of readings to be done by candidates for the ministry and courses to be taught on their behalf by Conference members. Followers of the Journal and the Conference could discover the theological directions and foundational studies minimally required of each minister. By the 1950's, however, the course of study listings were gone.

At no Conference level was the theological concern being monitored, it seems. As early as 1804, Bugbee says, the Quarterly Conference had become business meetings.[29] An efficient machinery was the hallmark of the denomination.[30] This became especially compelling at important turning points in Methodist history: the merger of three Methodist bodies in 1938 required the creation of a segregated Central Jurisdiction, which went unchanged for three decades. But even those who opposed it—such as Mark

Dawber, whose 1937 resolution expressed "regret that some more acceptable way was not provided to deal with the Negro situation"—looked to administrative rather than doctrinal prospects for facing the problem.[31] They wondered "what to do."

III

In a way, it is an odd story. For while Methodists were troubled only marginally about matters of doctrine, other heirs of John Wesley were very much concerned about his first Conference questions—"what to teach" and "how to teach." The Wesleyan Methodists stayed alert to the sanctification issue in the Founder's thought. And the United Brethren exercised a continuing theological vigilance. Their roots in the Heidelberg Catechism were no more important to Otterbein than were Cranmer's sermons on justification or the Articles of Religion to Wesley. But the ongoing theological responsibility of the Conference seems to have been taken more seriously by the continental ancestors of today's United Methodists. In 1815 in Conference, the United Brethren were writing a Discipline that began with doctrinal affirmations before it addressed polity concerns.[32] The 1889 Confession of Faith offered a doctrinal statement on sanctification, something which Methodists never saw fit to do despite the doctrine's importance for Wesley.[33]

Albright's Evangelicals, meanwhile, were also drafting theological statements, including an addition to the Methodist Episcopal Church's Articles in 1832 which proclaimed a doctrine of double judgment—the faithful to eternal life, and the ungodly to everlasting damnation.[34]

Over the years revisions continued, and as late as 1962 the Evangelical United Brethren Church was still engaged in Conference discussions of "what to teach."[35] Thus, by the era of the EUB—Methodist merger in 1968, Methodists were relative illiterates in theology, when compared to the minority with whom they were uniting.

An important illustration of the problem arose at the threshold of the merger. The first Restrictive Rule of the denomination forbade alteration of the Articles of Religion, in keeping with the Methodist custom of treating Wesley's doctrine as sacrosanct. Yet Wesley had no statement of double judgment, and the Evangelical United Brethren Church did. Could the merging bodies bring their doctrines together without violating the first Rule? The General Conference and the Judical Council, in an interesting act of ecclesiastical magic, determined that no conflict existed. Theology was subsumed under the category of polity.[38] The theological documents of both denominational traditions were published sequentially in the new United Methodist *Book of Discipline*, where they remain today.[39] And the existing ambiguity suggests an unhappy conclusion: that the Church considers theology irrelevant and is content to be "doctrinally incoherent," and that "the Church is now to live perpetually on theological credit."[40]

IV

To forestall that conclusion is the responsibility of the Conference: perhaps the General Conference, at its level, should create a board whose business it is to develop theological coherence for the denomination; but more to the point, it is the Annual Conference that most nearly institutionalizes the functions which Wesley had in mind, for the Annual Conference selects its ministers and supervises their training and bears the burden of initiating ministry in human communities. Unfortunately, the Annual Conference has continued to drift away from the first two questions—"What to teach?" and "How to teach?"—in a busy exercise over what to do.

There has been a loss of contact between the Conference and the issue of doctrinal integrity, even in symbolic ways. Since the Annual Conference Yearbook ceased publication of the course of study listings, only those who administer the course and those who sit on the Conference Board of the Ordained Ministry have any contact with the doctrinal content of candidates' preparation. The removal of the ministerial examinations from the time of Annual Conference sessions has physically and emotionally separated this aspect of theological responsibility from the Conference.

Some suspect that increased lay involvement in Methodist leadership encouraged this trend. Untrained laity could not be saddled with the burdens of theological sophistication, it would seem. Yet history suggests that this inference is misleading in two ways.

First, Wesley began his movement and watched his Conference grow with the involvement of lay preachers. The Conference emerged not as a graduate theological seminar but as a training opportunity for the unlearned. United Methodists still expect relatively untrained laity to handle teaching roles in Christian education, youth activities, and so on; but such doctrinal training as the Conference provides occurs in a casual way during workshops, which generally focus on "what to do" or "how to teach," rather than "what to teach." In any case, there is little institutional, doctrinal accountability to the Conference in such learning settings, for they are voluntary and vary in constituency from one occasion to the next. There are no longer any Conference certifications of Church School teachers,[41] and therefore no Conference incentives to reclaim theological integrity.

Second, lay involvement at the Annual Conference level is a much more recent phenomenon than our doctrinal indifference has been. Only in the late 19th century did lay men and women gain access to the General Conference. Lay Association meetings in the Wyoming Conference did not begin until 1905, with a session held at the First Presbyterian Church of West Pittston.[42] And only after the Uniting Conference of three Methodist bodies were lay delegates fully received into the Annual Conference sessions,[43] though Conference practice still excludes them from the arena where decisions about ministerial relationships (such as election to membership and ordination) are made.

So lay involvement is not the reason for our theological apathy. And therefore it should not be a barrier to the recovery of our two-hundred year-old task, to answer the question, "What to teach?"

Practical channels for the reclamation process are open: some, perhaps, fanciful; others practical; still others pastorally necessary, we may discover.

The Conference could adopt a procedure akin to the inaugural address used in political and academic circles, whereby a candidate at some point during his or her steps into ministry delivers a theological presentation to the Conference. Presently such statements are written and read by members (or a subcommittee) of the Board of Ordained Ministry. Greater care might be devoted by a candidate if he or she knew an audience of 400 would be listening and would use the presentation for theological dialogue and reflection.

The Conference could also recruit, from within or outside its own members, individuals who might offer the benefits of experienced theological reflection. Such persons' oral or written contributions could be inserted for structured discussion into the agenda—not as lectures which Conference delegates use as time to browse in the bookstore, but as documents which small groups throughout the Conference year discuss and evaluate.

The Conference could also take seriously the ecumenical opportunities it has for the theological dimensions of pastoral care. United Methodists need to be exposed to the fundamental doctrinal differences which our tradition has with groups as diverse as Mormons and Moonies. The levels of social acceptability which a religious group or cult has attained should not eliminate doctrine as a factor when we decide how to relate to it. United Methodists also need to move in ecumenical matters beyond such pleasantries as the typical preacher-priest combination in a Roman Catholic/United Methodist wedding. For years we have done that, but we have not pursued the theological implications of such activity: for example, the Roman Catholic and United Methodist Churches recognize the validity of each other's Baptisms, and a dispensation for inter-faith marriage can only be granted upon conditions that include proof of the non-Catholic partner's valid Baptism; but the children born to such an interfaith marriage cannot be baptized in any inter-faith ritual. Increasingly, United Methodist ministers will have to help their parishioners cope with that heretofore tolerated ambiguity. One mechanism for coping might lie in the creation of a theological dialogue on the Conference/Diocese level, reports upon which could be shared with the Annual Conference.

V

John Wesley was not indifferent to the pastoral, soul-saving ramifications of doctrine. But his ecclesiastical heirs have been. We have transmuted doctrine into matters of polity in hoping to answer the question, "What to do?" before addressing the first question, "What to teach?" Wesley's instrument for doctrinal exploration, the Conference, remains alive. But its theological task has been neglected, and its authority is eroding. That may not be just a coincidence.

END NOTES

1. George E. Ogle, "More at Stake than Tomatoes," *The Interpreter,* vol. 26, number 7 (September, 1982) pp. 19ff.

2. "The Doctrinal Minutes," or "Minutes of Several Late Conversations," in *The Works of the Rev. John Wesley* (London: Wesleyan Methodist Book Room, 1878) vol. VIII, p. 275.

3. "The Dogmatic Constitution on the Church," in *Vatican II: The Conciliar and Post-Conciliar Documents,* Austin Flannery, OP, editor. (Northport, New York: Costello Publishing Company, 1971) Chapter III.

"The bishops, as vicars and legates of Christ, govern the particular churches assigned to them by their counsels, exhortation, and example, but over and above that also by the authority and sacred power which indeed they exercise exclusively for the spiritual development of their flock in truth and holiness, keeping in mind that he who is greater should become as the lesser. . . . This power, which they exercise personally in the name of Christ, is proper, ordinary, and immediate, although its exercise is ultimately controlled by the supreme authority of the Church. . . . In virtue of this power bishops have a sacred right and duty before the Lord of legislating for and of passing judgment on their subjects . . ." (Section 27, pp. 382-383).

"The college or body of bishops has for all that no authority unless united with the Roman Pontiff . . . For the Roman Pontiff . . . has full, supreme, and universal power over the whole church, a power which he can always exercise unhindered." (Section 22, p. 375).

4. "The Dogmatic Constitution on the Church," paragraphs 21 and 41, in Walter M. Abbott, S. J., *The Documents of Vatican II*. Chicago: Association Press. 1966. pp. 40, 68. Cf. Flannery, *op. cit.,* editor, pp. 372, 386, 398.

5. Paul McCleary, "Authority Centers in United Methodism," *The Christian Advocate,* vol. XV, no. 13, pp. 11-12.

6. Frederick A. Norwood, *The Story of American Methodism: A History of the United Methodists and Their Relations* (Nashville: Abingdon, 1974), pp. 17, 124-125.

7. *Ibid.,* p. 125.

8. *Ibid.,* p. 124. Cf. David Sherman, *History of the Revisions of the Discipline of the Methodist Episcopal Church* (New York: Nelson and Phillips. 1874), p. 27.

9. Sherman, *op. cit.,* p. 28.

10. *Ibid.,* p. 30. Norwood, *op. cit.,* p. 133.

11. McCleary, *op. cit.,* p. 12.

12. Quoted in Norwood, *op. cit.,* pp. 124-125.

13. McCleary, *op. cit.,* p. 12.

14. Norwood, *op. cit.,* p. 17.

15. See, for example, the following Conference *Yearbooks:* 1934, p. 318; 1935, pp. 543 and 549; 1945, p. 91; 1951, p. 710.

16. From data of one group of problem pregnancy counselors in the early 1970's.

17. *The New York Times,* September 14, 1981, p. B2.

18. *The Spark,* Wyoming Conference edition of *The United Methodist Reporter,* December 4, 1981, p. 1.

19. Sherman, *op. cit.,* pp. 68-69.

20. "The Large Minutes," in *The Works of the Rev. John Wesley, A. M.* (London: Wesleyan Methodist Book Room) 1878) vol VIII, p. 313.

21. Albert C. Outler, *John Wesley* (New York: Oxford University Press, 1964), p. 134.

22. *Ibid.,* p. 135.

23. Norwood, *op. cit.,* p. 99.

24. *Ibid.,* p. 225.

25. *Ibid.,* p. 226.

26. *Ibid.,* p. 196.

27. Leroy Bugbee, *He Holds the Stars in His Hands: The Centennial History of the Wyoming Conference of the Methodist Church,* 1852-1952 (Scranton: Wyoming Annual Conference, 1952), pp. 5-7, 13.

28. *Ibid.,* p. 40.

29. *Ibid.,* p. 16.

30. *Ibid.,* p. 15.

31. *The Yearbook,* Wyoming Annual Conference of the Methodist Episcopal Church, 1937, p. 24.

32. Kenneth Rowe, "Our Four Confessions of Faith," unpublished paper distributed for class use at Drew University. Cf. Norwood, *op. cit.,* p. 108.

33. Rowe, *ibid.,* pp. 1-2. (Methodist Protestants had one, but the 1938 Uniting Conference did not vote upon its inclusion as an Article of Religion in The Methodist Church. The same Conference did, however, vote an allegiance of all Christians to civil authority.)

34. *Ibid.,* p. 4.

35. Norwood, *op. cit.,* pp. 427ff.

36. *Ibid.,* p. 428.

37. *Doctrines and Discipline of the Methodist Church.* Nashville: Methodist Publishing House. 1964. p. 16.

38. Robert E. Cushman, "Church Doctrinal Standards Today," *Religion in Life,* vol. 44 (Winter, 1975), p. 401.

39. *The Book of Discipline of the United Methodist Church.* Nashville: The United Methodist Publishing House. 1980. pp. 55-68.

40. Cushman, *op. cit.,* pp. 401-402. For the concept of living on the credit of theological capital of the past, see John B. Cobb, Jr., *Liberal Christianity at the Crossroads* (Philadelphia: Westminster Press, 1973).

40. See the *Yearbook* of Wyoming Conference, 1931, pp. 535f.

42. Bugbee, *op. cit.,* p. 271.

43. *Ibid.,* p. 273.

PREACHER'S WIFE

Glenda L. Taylor

> Miss Severson said she believed God wanted me to be a minister's wife. I replied, "Oh, no, not a minister's wife, anything but that! I'll go to China or India if he leads me there, but not a preacher's wife. It's the most thankless task anyone could have, I think."

Thus began Anna's reluctant entry into a lifetime of service to her church and its people in the role of "preacher's wife." Anna Jurisch and Benjamine Hanton were united in marriage on July 8, 1897, near Susquehanna, Pennsylvania; and as she later noted in her memoirs, "together started in the ministry of the dear old Wyoming Conference of the Methodist Church." *

Her young husband was an English immigrant full of determination and a zest to serve. His enthusiasm was contagious to his new bride. Her own words reflect their idealism:

> At the wedding ceremony my pastor in congratulating us said, "I wish you much happiness and good charges." We thanked him but answered him and said we were not so anxious about the good charges but wanted to go where we were needed most and where the Lord could use us to serve Him best. Our hearts were enthusiastic and ready to take the hard places where the need was the greatest. So we had been appointed by the Conference to what was called by some of the preachers "the preacher's calf pasture," where the young preachers were broken in to become used to hardship and hard work.

Married for only one day, the new bride plunged into the "calf pasture" with all the courage she could muster. They traveled by train to their new parish in Rowlands, where they were met at the station by a friend. Anna tried to hide her dismay as she eyed their means of transportation. She had been expecting a horse and buggy but managed to hide her disappointment and smile as she was lifted up to the great high seat of an old farm wagon.

Upon this conspicuous perch they were driven through the small town. She clutched the precarious seat and tried to concentrate on her new surroundings. She spotted the tiny church with its spire pointing determinedly heavenward. It was not an imposing edifice, she decided, but the sight of it gave her some comfort. (She was later to develop a fondness for its small bell which tolled with a sound that seemed to suggest it would be more at home around a cow's neck.)

The short journey was taking on frightening dimensions as they rattled along the rough road, and she felt something akin to stage fright. She remembers:

> I was wondering if there would be anybody to see us—just hoping not for the time being to look at and judge the bride. Benjamine had been on the charge for over three

months, so they had summed him up, but poor ME! As we passed a house here and there on the way the curtains would be pulled aside, and we could see a face or two watching. I was so nervous and sensitive over it that my spirits were very low by the time we reached the little story and a half canal house which was to be our future home.

This, their first residence together, was located along a towpath to the canal. It was a simple and modest place, in keeping with the humble lifestyle expected of the religious example of the church. A gesture had been made to welcome the newlyweds. Awaiting them, Anna recalls, was:

> . . . a nice cake, a pan of fresh eggs (on which our friend George had written something funny on each one), a pat of butter, and a loaf of homemade bread. So our first meal consisted of bread and butter, eggs, and cake. Neither of us were very hungry—just wishing we could be alone awhile, as we were both very tired; but, like preacher's folk, we could not stop to think of what we wanted but tried to adjust ourselves to the plans of our parishioners. We got ourselves together to meet our new church family.
>
> We had just one lamp as many of our belongings had not arrived, of course, so we had to make out with the few little things we had on hand which were few and very limited.
>
> Early in the evening our guests began to arrive. As we had only about a half dozen chairs, some of the men and ladies began figuring ways to take care of the numbers they knew were coming. They borrowed lamps from our only near neighbors. Some had brought lamps with them. The men got boxes and boards, placing them around the room which, with the few chairs, furnished a place to sit.

The warm welcome helped, but that was social. There was still an official role to fill. Anna writes:

> I shall never forget my first Sunday as a minister's wife. Benjamine had gone (walked) two miles up the twopath to his morning service at Hamar's school house. I was to meet him at the church for the early afternoon service at Rowland, after which we had Sunday School. I went in and sat near the front where the parsonage family usually sits. Not a soul spoke to me. I will confess that I was a bit homesick and lonely. I was enthusiastic and anxious to get started in the work. Everything was strange and different to me. I felt that I was under inspection and wished I could just drop out of sight. But just before the service Mrs. Griswold, a dear motherly soul, came and sat with me which helped lift my spirits.

She felt she was over the hurdle; and by the time the spire sang with its cow-bell voice, she was reasonably sure this little "preacher's wife" was going to do just fine. But after the service everyone simply left with few words or signs of welcome for her. She refused to be disheartened so soon, however, and decided upon a different approach:

> I realized afterwards that they were a bit backward and timid, and I would have to be the one to break the ice—to make the advances. After the first Sunday I always met them at the door with my husband, shook their hands, and welcomed them to the service and very soon was at home with them and learned to love them dearly.

Anna's first efforts were mostly among the youth of the church and community. Little organized work had been done for the young people, and her first step was to form an Epworth League. Most of the responsibility of this work fell to her because Benjamine had many other services on various other points of the charge.

The group flourished, and Anna would have felt satisfied with the results it it hadn't been for two teenage boys who were posing a problem at the evening preaching service. They teased the girls, threw spit balls, and made so much noise no one could concentrate on what the preacher was saying.

Benjamine tried kindness and patience with them to no avail. Finally, after one particularly disruptive service, he called them aside. "Now boys I want you at church," he told them, "but you will either come and behave yourselves or stay away. This is the house of God, and I cannot and will not tolerate any irreverence. I am interested in you and want you here if you can come and behave and realize that this is the house of God, not the town hall. Either this or I'll have to use more strenuous measures. I mean what I say!"

The reprimand sparked their anger, and they left in a flurry of dramatics. "We'll never darken the door of the church while that snip of a preacher is there," they swore and then added in further retaliation, "nor speak to him!"

They held firm to their vow, and when they would chance to meet the Hantons on the street their pointed "Good morning, MRS. Hanton," reinforced their point while Benjamine's greetings continued to meet stone-faced silence.

This was a source of some amusement to the young minister and his wife, as well as a concern. They were too busy to dwell on it, however, for they were occupied with a tiny daughter born in November of 1898 at the start of an unusually severe winter.

One March day when it seemed winter's grasp should be slackening, a fit of arctic fury stormed into their area. Snow, whipped by bitter winds, rose high into the air and swirled across fields like dizzy ghosts.

Benjamine was worried. Their dwindling coal supply was down to one small pailful scraped from the recesses of the coal bin. Money was even more scarce. He used what little they possessed to purchase food to last them throughout the storm. As much as it hurt to do so, he sent word to Mr. Griswold, the church treasurer, asking for an advance on his salary in order to purchase a ton of coal. Their coal, however, needed to be hauled from a town about ten miles away, and no one could get through the high drifts which covered the road.

What were they going to do, they wondered. Anna hovered anxiously over Baby Vera and moved her small bed a little closer to the old pot-bellied stove. She hung a blanket over the parlor's archway in an attempt to lessen the area they needed to heat. Benjamine, in the meantime, took an ax and made his way along the river bank to where a dead apple tree stood.

The following morning as they knelt for their morning devotions a firm "Whoa!" interrupted their prayers of supplication. Rising, they rushed to the door to see the station agent with his horse and sleigh. Accompanying him were the two teenagers and three burlap bags of coal which they shoveled into the basement.

As the two youths hung back in embarrassment, the station agent
delighted in telling their story. They had walked past the parsonage to visit
the Griswold family early that morning.

"Gee, it looks awful cold down to the preacher's," they remarked,
"couldn't see through the windows as they're all covered with ice and snow.
Wonder if they have plenty of coal?"

Mr. Griswold told them how Rev. Hanton had tried to get coal, but the
storm had grown too severe, and the roads could not be traveled.

Back home they trudged and told everyone they could find of the parsonage family's plight. They scooped up coal from their own bins and raised
enough money to buy another ton, which they planned to fetch as soon as the
team could get through. They even had $3 left over and gave it to Benjamine
to buy food.

The aroma of apple wood embers filled the cramped parlor, but the
warmth seemed to be radiating from within as the story unfolded. Benjamine
knew next Sunday would find two familiar faces back in the congregation,
minus the spit balls.

> Oh, what lessons of faith and trust I learned in those early days of our ministry. So
> many times all I could count on was my faith in His care and guidance. I was naturally a
> rather timid soul, never having been alone in my life and always having been abundantly
> provided for. This all took faith and courage, which my Heavenly Father provided.

Perhaps the most difficult obstacle for Anna to overcome was fear. Their
small house along the canal was somewhat isolated, and at dusk the shadowy
surroundings took on frightening shapes. What the eerie setting didn't
provide to encourage panic, her vivid imagination did.

> At first we were unable to purchase window shades, so before darkness settled down,
> I would go outside and close all the shutters to protect myself, when alone, from peering
> eyes. This task I did in fear and trembling, as tramps were so frequent; we never knew
> when one might be prowling around. I always had a feeling while outside that someone
> would grab me.
>
> I had to be alone so much, especially nights, when Benjamine would have to be at his
> outer preaching places. These nights I would look after our youth group at the home
> church. On one occasion I had returned from the church and was sitting by the table
> reading while waiting for Benjamine's return. Suddenly a man's hand reached through
> the shutters of the front window, the fingers trying to reach the hook that fastened them. I
> saw the hand, but I did not move or let on that I noticed anything. I kept my eyes on my
> book. Afraid? Yes! But I lifted my heart in prayer and asked God to make me brave and
> to take care of me. Fear left me and so did the hand in the shutter. I do not know who it
> was, nor his intentions, but whoever it was just left with no sound or trouble. Soon I
> heard familiar footsteps—Benjamine was home and we both were safe for our Heavenly
> Father's presence was there with us. How often He proved His watchful care over us!

The summertime practice of camp meetings played an important part in
the lives of these turn-of-the-century Methodists. Its informal setting was rich
in spiritual renewal, fellowship, and just plain fun.** Anna fondly remembers one incident:

> It was my husband's night to preach, and during his sermon he mentioned his hav-
> ing to change his clothes three times one Sunday as it had been a day of showers. Coming
> from his early morning service four miles from home, he got soaked from one shower. He

changed, and I dried and pressed his clothes, as in the afternoon he had to preach at another point and again in the evening at another. I had the suit dried and ready, but on his way home he again got wet in another shower. The third time, coming from his evening service at Lackawaxen several miles from home (he had to walk as he had no conveyance at that time), he got drenched again. Three times he changed that day.

Dr. Woodruff said after the sermon that he could not imagine a Methodist preacher having three suits of clothes to change with, and he must look into it and perhaps have his salary reduced. Of course, this caused a big laugh, but Benjamine said, "My good wife saved the day for me—me and my one Sunday suit."

The Hanton family was completed with the birth of a second daughter, Marjorie, in 1905 at Jackson. Anna's memoirs are rich in stories about her children:

How well I remember my daughter's (Vera) first appearance in public as a singer! She was about four years old, and it was Children's Day. The altar rail was trimmed with greens and flowers. In the center of the altar trimming was a lovely, large rose. She was to sing her little song (I was at the organ accompanying her) when partly through her song, she spied the rose, stopped in the midst of it, went down and smelled the rose, went back to her place on the platform, and finished her song. This caused quite a laugh and clapping of hands, which rather embarrassed her.

We always looked forward to the Quarterly Conference. We had planned at one of these Conferences to have Vera baptized. It was at the Sunday morning service. I had previously explained the meaning of it as best I could, so she in her little mind could grasp somewhat of its meaning. I told her just what Rev. Warner would do and why. Her father and I were at the altar with her, and while the service was being read, she got a bit restless. Looking up into Rev. Warner's face, she said, "Well, if you're going to do it, do it." So with a smile he did it.

When her father had been away and returned home, Vera would always be watching for him. As she ran to meet him he would stretch out his arms and say, "Come into my arms like a bundle of charms and stick to my heart like putty." The revival meetings had inspired her to hold an altar service for her dolls one day, and I found her with all her dolls on their knees in front of the lounge where she was teaching them Bible verses. To her favorite rag doll, Angie, she said, "Now Angie, repeat this after me until you learn it: Suffer the little children to come unto me, and stick to my heart like putty."

One of the most difficult aspects of the Methodist ministry is its itineracy. Constantly moving about from pastorate to pastorate causes a lot of wear and tear on furniture and even more on heartstrings. The fragile china, packed in a barrel, and the heart, heavy at bidding a tearful farewell at the train station—both suddenly seem so breakable. And then there's all those new people to meet. . . .

As I think of the different charges, the faces and experiences come back to me so plainly. . . . the welcomes we received. . . . those welcoming receptions where we were put up front or on the church platforms for inspection (or so we felt). How the girls always dreaded it. They felt so conspicious and nervous, but the hearts of our people were warm and kindly.

On one charge there was no parsonage, and a house was rented for a home for the preacher's family. The house was small, and being in a mining town, the cellar floor was damp and wet from the dirty black water seeping in. We had to lay boards from one part to another on which to walk. There was no bathroom, but down in this wet musty basement a partition enclosed a space large enough for an old tin bathtub. I felt sure we would all have typhoid or something else from these conditions.

While waiting for our goods to arrive, sitting on the bed upstairs . . . on the bare mattress . . . and being so discouraged and upset, Marjorie looked out the window and spied a boy about her own age. "Look, Mother!" she cried, "There's a boy across the street, and he looks quite sanitary." She and John soon became good friends.

After getting all cleaned and settled, our night soon became disturbed by intruders. We discovered, on examination, that once more in our itineracy we were invaded by bed-bugs! These beds had been donated by parishioners, none were new. Here is where I almost lost my religion! This seemed to be the last straw. We burned the mattresses and soaked the beds with boiling water and turpentine.

People tend to expect a lot of perfection from the individuals who live in their parsonage, sometimes to the point of denying their humanness. This can be a very uncomfortable way to live, expecially when the judgement is self-inflicted.

I had many struggles with my inner self. Things occurred among some of our church members which caused me to lose faith in them. I became discouraged and at times felt such a failure. At times I would become despondent and feel that I was no real Christian. I would at times become irritable and impatient, which I knew was unchristian. My health was not too good, which did not help the situation any, and I even told Benjamine that I could not go to prayer meeting for the folks would expect me to pray, and I could not for it would be hypocritical. I told him I was going to write to my friends and tell them I was no Christian, and they must not expect anything from me anymore. What a struggle I had, but alone in my room on my knees, God spoke peace to my troubled soul, and the struggle was over. God won out that time. I had lost faith (so I thought and said) in everyone save the Lord. But that, too, was restored, and I realized how very human we all are. Even ministers and their families have their inward struggles and battles themselves.

The Reverend Hanton retired in 1941 after 53 years of active service in Wyoming Conference. And his wife, did she have any regrets? After she recorded her initial outburst at the thought of being a minister's wife, she went on to write: "But how wrong, how very wrong I was. Later there was nothing I would rather be. In all the years in the work with my dear husband I never had a regret or would I change for any other life." It wasn't China or India, but rather Wyoming Conference that needed her—this little "preacher's wife."

*This is Anna Hanton's story, told with her own words as much as possible. One of Mrs. Hanton's gifts to the future was an autobiographical manuscript, complete with self-drawn illustrations. She has preserved a warm, generous slice of human interest, and her memoirs deserve to be read.

Another of her contributions to posterity is her daughter, Marjorie; and it is to her we owe our gratitude for sharing her mother's manuscript. The Rev Marjorie Hanton is a retired deaconess of Wyoming Conference and now lives in Tunkhannock, PA.

**Serving in the ministry had its lighter side too.

"BITS AND PIECES OF HISTORY"

History is constituted by great movements, critical events, and significant people. Often, however, as our eyes take in the great panorama, we fail to see the details. Following are some "bits and pieces" constituting some of those particulars, in the history of the Wyoming Conference.

PRAYERS, PENNIES, AND PERSEVERANCE:
WOMEN'S WORK IN THE WYOMING CONFERENCE

Grace Terwillinger

In the ensuing paragraphs are some small slices of history that describe some of the early work of the women of the churches of the Wyoming Conference—a wide variety of information recently provided by persons in those churches, in response to a broadcast request for information.

In the early years of the Methodist Church, women held neither vote nor office. Church minutes from those years accord women no acclaim for duties well done, no thanks for hours of service for the Kingdom. Nevertheless, the women accepted their culturally-defined role: they put on dinners, quilted, helped to pay the pastor, kept the parsonage comfortable, and cared for the sick, the poor, and the dying.

Women gradually began to break out of the shell of social insecurity, which had so long kept them from ministering to some of the uncared-for needs of the world. They also became aware of the suffering outside the four walls of their church buildings. They heard, from some of the missionaries, of the great misery in the Orient. They were appalled to learn that there were places where little girls were considered surplus and drowned at birth, where thousands of little girls were dedicated to lives of slavery under the name of religion, where girls were locked into harems for their whole lives. Women and children were in need of physicians, but how could a doctor preach the gospel, or cure the sick, in countries where women covered their faces and fled from men? Women, and only women, with God's help, could change those patterns of life.

The information received has been classified according to the predecessor organizations of the Women's Society of Christian Service, and the present United Methodist Women: the Women's Foreign Missionary Society, the Wesleyan Service Guild, the Women's Home Missionary Society, and the Ladies Aid.

1. Women's Foreign Missionary Society

The first Women's Foreign Missionary Society in the Wyoming Conference was organized under the jurisdiction of the New York Branch:

> The meeting was held June 8, 1870, in the Centenary Church, Binghamton, N. Y., it being the only Methodist Church in Binghamton. Mrs. William Butler, who was one of the Boston Charter Members, attended the meeting. She also came to confer with the pastor, Dr. Olin, regarding the appointment of Miss Fannie Sparks as a missionary woman.[1]

In October of 1870, Miss Sparks sailed for India, giving Wyoming Conference the honor of furnishing the first missionary to be sent from the New York Branch of the Women's Foreign Missionary Society.

On March 22, 1870, the Philadelphia Branch of the W. F. M. S. was organized, encompassing the states of Pennsylvania, Delaware, and New York. Wyoming Conference, thus, became part of both the Philadelphia and New York Branches.

The minutes of the Seventieth Annual Report of the Philadelphia Branch of the W. F. M. S. contain this account of the first Wyoming Conference organization in the Philadelphia Branch:

> The Ladies of the Congregation connected with the Methodist Episcopal Church of Providence, Pa. met at 3 o'clock October 5, 1870, pursuant to appointment, in the audience room of said Church for the purpose of organizing a Female Missionary Society ... The First Missionary sent from this out by this fractional group was Miss Ida Walton, who went to Mexico in 1890 to teach in the mission school.[2]

A period of stable growth began along northern Pennsylvania and southern New York for the W. F. M. S. With the help and interest of church groups in the cities of Wilkes-Barre and Scranton, the Philadelphia Branch grew much faster than the New York Branch. By 1892, there were eighty-four auxiliaries and bands. Income, however, was small, and progress was slow. Meetings were sporadically attended, sometimes by only two or three, and other times by thirty or more. In spite of small collections, the women were undaunted, and the group's progress continued.

Mission Schools and Bible Women were being supported by women's groups by the early 1900's. In 1903, some thirty-four societies in Wyoming Conference were supporting such work: one in China, one in Japan, three in Korea, one in Malaya, two in Mexico, twenty-four in India, and two in Italy. Scholarship support and orphan sponsorship became important areas of concern. To give some idea of the costs involved, care of an orphan for a year ranged from twenty dollars in India, to eighty-three dollars in South America. Likewise, the support of a Bible Woman varied country to country, with $220.00 per year usually the maximum.[3]

The majority of churches in New York State aided the work in India, providing five Mission School scholarships and support for two orphans and one Bible Woman. Individual churches also had their unique projects:

OWEGO provided a scholarship in Peking, and ONEONTA a scholarship in Japan.

The King's Daughters of TABERNACLE CHURCH, BINGHAMTON, provided a scholarship for Nagasaki, Japan.

SIDNEY supported an orphan in Foochow, China. Later, they supported the Gardens, who were missionaries in India. The Gardens visited Sidney, and the W. F. M. S., hearing of the extensive area the Gardens cared for, decided to raise enough money to buy a car for their work. The men of the church became interested, and a new Ford was purchased and shipped to India for the Gardens' use.

In COOPERSTOWN, the W. F. M. S. was organized on October 2, 1901. After the ladies had listened to a report from the Annual Meeting of the New York Branch, Mrs. Littell was elected the first President. The work in India became their first concern. Dues of five cents per member, and mite boxes given out, helped to provide financial support. They made a quilt, then set out to find a family in need, to whom to give that quilt. (This was perhaps the first recorded act of Home Mission in the Wyoming Conference.) They were asked to accept a share of funding for Charlotte Jewel in Peking, China. Each District of the W. F. M. S. was asked to contribute toward the six hundred dollars needed for her support. A collection was taken, but only forty cents were collected. In 1903, they studied Africa and collected $4.24. In 1902, they organized a children's society, "Mother's Jewels." In 1909, a letter was received, asking for a collection to help close the doors of the Knickerbocker Trust Company, which held $20,000 belonging to the Foreign Missionary Society. Minutes of September 1, 1902, recorded, "Decided to provide tea and wafers as a *mental refreshment* for the meetings."

DORRANCETON CHURCH began its W. F. M. S. in November of 1897, the church itself having been established only three years earlier. Very successful through the years, in 1922-1924, they had 154 members and gave $2,030 to missions, supporting a scholarship and a Bible Woman in Korea. They also sent money to Blanch Search in China and Ethel Miller in Korea.

From ATHENS, PENNSYLVANIA, we have a picture of Mrs. Myra Park Tracy, who went to Turkey as a missionary. She was the first scholar from the Athens Methodist Sunday School to enter foreign mission work. Athens began supporting a girl in Bacoda Mission School in India in 1900 for fifteen dollars per year, a project they continued for several years. In 1904, minutes relate the names of several missionaries having labored in the Chinese field—Miss Walston, Mrs. King, Mrs. Elizabeth Brewster—leaving their homes, families, comfort, and safety.

FRANKLIN FORKS formed their Society following the famine of 1861 in India. In 1884, Mrs. E. L. Beebe and Mrs. S. L. Stockwell re-organized missionary interest into the W. F. M. S. Mite boxes and missionary barrels not only increased giving, but also made many people conscious of mission needs around the world.

In CASTLE CREEK the minutes record that the women were making bloomers to send to women in Italy.

ONEONTA—The first existing record indicates the W. F. M. S. was active in 1875. In that year, they paid the Conference $7.95. However, the group grew over the years, and by 1924, they gave $1,328 to the Conference. The Oneonta W. F. M. S. and W. H. M. S. were both handsomely remembered in the wills of Mrs. Samuel Borst and Mrs. Seward Terry. A portion of Mrs. Borst's bequest built a school for girls in Puerto Rico.

From the minutes of an ONEONTA DISTRICT meeting in Sunday: "Opened the meeting with worship service and an anecdote, 'Tipping the Plank.' When the plank was tipped across a muddy stream it disclosed innumerable repulsive things not visible before. This illustrates conditions in foreign lands (as well as at home) which do not appear on the surface, but which are revolting and lamentable. The plank *must* be tipped and the repulsive things destroyed." Three hundred sixty-one members were reported, with 134 mite boxes returned. There were also the following reports:

> The Queen Esthers of SHERBURNE reported they had raised $94.02 by food sales and other means and had sent two barrels of clothing. They are also helping to educate a little colored girl whose mother died.
> NORWICH reported thirty-nine paid members, sent dues of $45.22 to Conference; mite boxes brought $25.00, self-denial, $14.00.
> UNADILLA reported twenty-seven members, sent three sacks of clothing and 124 garments to Ellis Island. They raised $8.03 with a supper, plus dues of $28.30. Mite boxes brought $4.50; freight on sacks was $.75 each. Queen Esther group raised $4.85; for stricken Belgium, $5.50. Total raised was $65.88.

At the District meeting, it was voted that at the Camp Meeting at Sidney Grove, one afternoon be devoted to a program by the Women's Foreign Missionary Society, and another to the Women's Home Missionary Society, with a paid speaker. From the platform, it was stated emphatically that "Oneonta District can do anything they want to; the point is 'TO WANT TO'. An office is not an honor; it is a responsibility." Officers elected were: President; First and Second Vice-Presidents; Evangelism, Young People's Work, Literature, Mite Boxes, Children's Work, Tithing Coordinators; a Press Secretary; and a Vice-President-at-Large. There was also a report on Folkes Institute, with high praise for the excellent work with girls in factories. Though they are there to study for mission work, it is good training—even if they do not go into the mission field.

From the LAKEVILLE CHURCH we have a message from a missionary teacher, Helen Gow, daughter of Rev. Gow, pastor of Lakeville Church 1928 to 1932. She writes that she was a missionary teacher for seventeen years with the Berean Mission in Zaire, Africa. She writes of the pleasure there when boxes of medical supplies, school supplies, and the very important gift of money to help the many needs, were received. She prays that the mission work would be blessed, as it continues ministering to the lost and needy people of Africa.

The LEHMAN CHURCH had both a W. F. M. S. and a W. H. M. S. meeting on the same day, one in the morning, the other in the afternoon.

Study books were used to learn about mission. Money was accrued by donations. In 1916, the Lehman Church had a Missionary Rally, featuring a missionary from Korea, Mr. Pyeng Oak Cho, as speaker.

In ENDWELL in 1938, a Women's Home and Foreign Missionary Society was organized, as well as a Queen Esther Auxiliary. Dues were one dollar per member and $.20 contingent fund. The church at that time eliminated all commercial projects and voted to devote their time to a Missionary Society. The question arose, "Just when and who ever made the rule that the women must help pay the minister, put on the suppers, care for the parsonage, and do all the other things they were expected to do?"

In the Conference itself, the first Standard Bearers Society for girls fourteen years of age was organized in the early 1900's and soon had 698 members. The King's Heralds, for girls 9 to 13, and the Little Light Bearers also became active groups of young people and were organized around 1905. They held meetings, usually in the homes, and studied various countries, usually choosing a missionary with whom to correspond, and receiving much-prized letters in return. They met at least twice a month, paid dues of two cents, and raised money in various ways to aid the mission work they studied. Ice cream socials were very popular, and in one community, a farmer harvested ice just for those summer festivals.

A Children's Band was organized May 11, 1875, in SUSQUEHANNA, PENNSYLVANIA. These became very popular young people's auxiliaries. Later, they became Young People's Bands, Royal Daughters, and later, Standard Bearers. So many names for similar groups caused great confusion. Conference action urged, as far as possible, for the sake of uniformity, the names of Standard Bearers, King's Heralds, and Little Light Bearers be used.

One of the most important factors in the success of the Standard Bearers was the founding of Camp Inspiration, using the Y. W. C. A. camp facilities at Lake Ariel. The girls attended classes, with missionaries present; many of these girls left camp dedicated and inspired to give their lives to mission work. During its existence, more than 1,000 girls attended Camp Inspiration. Forty-seven dedicated their lives to the church, and many new Societies were organized. Three of the girls became foreign missionaries, and two, home missionaries. In 1923, Miss Florence Sweet sailed for China, having been profoundly influenced by her stay at Camp Inspiration.

Women's Foreign Missionary Societies were also organized in Simpson, Pennsylvania, on September 1, 1874; at First Church, Endicott, in 1911; and at West Pittston, Pennsylvania, in 1874.

In the early days of the Society, the slogan and pledge of the members was, "Two cents a week, and a prayer." The dues were one dollar a year. Dues were supplemented by tithes, offerings, annuities, bequests, and memorials. Sixty thousand members, by 1923, pledged one-tenth of their income to the Society. Twenty-four thousand women were members of the League of Intercessors, who prayed for divine guidance and help. In 1923, the appropriation totalled $2,350,276.00. There were no salaried officers in the Women's Foreign Missionary Society.

The last recorded meeting of the W. F. M. S. was held at Camp Inspiration on June 26, 1940. The seventy years of their existence had been marked by struggle, overcome by perseverance. They had raised over $61,000,000.00 through dues, mite boxes, and various types of membership—not a bad record at all.

The endeavors of hundreds of women in the work of the Women's Foreign Missionary Society and its auxiliaries brought love and care to millions around the world.

2. Wesleyan Service Guild

Just as the Civil War had engendered many changes in the status of women, so too did the First World War. Women became community workers and business managers in industry and the professions. Although unable to attend meetings of mission-related groups during the day, many of these working women were nonetheless interested in the church's mission work.

With these women in mind, the Wesleyan Service Guild was organized in 1916, as an auxiliary to both the W. F. M. S. and the W. H. M. S. It was a success almost from the start.

By 1930, the Guild was supporting five missionaries, had 3,666 members (420 in Wyoming Conference), and was performing needed work in the mission field.

3. Women's Home Missionary Society

In April, 1883, the Women's Home Missionary Society for Wyoming Conference was organized at Centenary Church, Binghamton, some three years after the founding of the national W. H. M. S. Bishop Wiley presided at that session of Annual Conference.

By 1892, Scranton and Wilkes-Barre had full-time city missionaries, and Binghamton soon followed. Foreign immigration of miners and industrial laborers brought increasing need for this type of ministry.

In 1893, the Wyoming Conference was able to give the national W. H. M. S. $2,055, the largest amount of any Conference. That same year, they supported two girls, one in Tivoli, New York, and the other at the Bennett Home in Mississippi. Boxes of clothing were sent, and a sewing machine purchased and shipped to the Industrial Home in Clarkson, Mississippi.

At the twenty-fifth anniversary of the W. H. M. S., in 1905, a silver offering of $2.50 per member was taken, and $9,000.00 were collected from Wyoming Conference. In 1907, special work with Italians in Pennsylvania was initiated by the Kingston W. H. M. S. In 1913, the Conference reported ten companies of Home Guards, with 239 members; twenty-four bands of Mother's Jewels, with 1,371 members; eighty auxiliaries, with 632 members; and Queen Esther Circles, with 3,011 members.

Through the years, a number of new projects were initiated. From the Deaconess Home in Binghamton evolved the Children's Home, which was incorporated in 1920. In the Queen Esther Circles, stewardship and tithing were encouraged, and by 1926, there were said to be 677 tithers in the Conference.

The Junior work was organized in 1881 by the national W. H. M. S. and became an important home missions thrust. The first unit recorded in Wyoming Conference was at Tabernacle Church, Binghamton. The group moved from Mother's Jewels, for children seven years old or under, to Home Guards, for children up to twelve years of age. Money was raised for various institutions, including the Jessie Lee Home in Seward, Alaska; the Mother's Jewels Home, at York, Nebraska; the Robinson Orphanage in Puerto Rico; and an orphanage in Louisiana.

Other groups throughout the Conference approached Home Mission in a variety of ways:

NORWICH, NEW YORK, and SIMPSON, PENNSYLVANIA, shared the honor of being the two Societies in the Wyoming Conference to meet the goal "Standards" for a year. Wyoming Conference was, for three years, the winning Conference for the Radio Complete Societies award. The award was to send a girl to the Jubilee Meeting in Cincinnati, with all expenses paid by the national-level Society. Since both Norwich and Simpson were equally honored in the Conference, two girls were sent, one from each church, one as Miss Cincinnati, the other, and Miss Wyoming (because her expenses were paid by the Conference).

CENTRAL CHURCH, ENDICOTT, received an award of five dollars for the best Digest of the Study Book, "Blind Spots." Several other Wyoming Conference Societies also received awards. The young people's interest stemmed, not only from studying about people, but also from doing something worthwhile themselves.

The Home Missionary Society in WEST PITTSTON was organized in 1886; Mrs. Janet McTee left a one thousand dollar bequest to Wood Junior College, in Mississippi, for purchasing a chapel organ. The Queen Esthers were very active. The Children's Home Missionary Society was started as "The Busy Bees Mission Board," with the older girls as "The Helping Hand Mission Board."

In 1938, ENDWELL CHURCH voted to eliminate all commercial projects, as noted above. Here, too, the Queen Esther Society was very active.

The DORRANCETON W. H. M. S. was organized in 1919. They are recorded as sponsoring Queen Esthers and Mother's Little Jewels. Two young women are reported as entering full-time mission service from this church: Florence Kaup, who became a Deaconess, and Phoebe Geyer, who was Superintendent of the Home Missionary Society in New York City.

COOPERSTOWN reports in 1922 both the W. F. M. S. and the W. H. M. S., as well as an active Ladies Aid, holding their meetings on the same day, but separately, often with dinner together. In 1922, they voted to continue this practice, with a program shared jointly by all three groups.

The SIDNEY CHURCH W. H. M. S. sponsored active Queen Esthers, sending girls to camp, and also sponsored Home Guards and Mother's Jewels. The Navajo Indians became one of their priorities, for both material assistance and personal contact. The W. H. M. S. in Sidney was the largest in Oneonta District. Their motto was, "For Love of Christ and His Name;" their goal, "To Help Win America for Christ."

DAMASCUS has a record of monies sent to the Home Missionary Society, though apparently it was not organized as such.

ATHENS Home Missionary Society was organized February 1, 1903, under the direction of Mrs. Bass, a national organizer. In 1905, it was reported that the Mother's Jewels collected money to buy gifts for each child in the Mother's Jewels Home at York, Nebraska, an orphanage of one hundred orphans, who were cared for directly by this Society.

In the 1906 Minutes of the Twenty-Fifth Anniversary Meeting in Binghamton, it was reported that forty industrial homes, twenty-eight deaconess homes, and four hospitals had been built, among other W. H. M. S. projects.

CASTLE CREEK Women's Home Missionary Society was meeting monthly in 1933, with a roll of twenty-two members.

In 1924, HUNTSVILLE Methodist Women organized with thirty charter members. Their Queen Esther Auxiliary sent a girl to camp each year. They also won an honorable mention for 100% plus, in subscriptions to the "Women's Home Missionary Magazine."

HONESDALE, PENNSYLVANIA reports that a Home Missionary Society was begun in January, 1903, by the previously-mentioned Mrs. Bass, from Syracuse. Early projects were missionary barrels of clothing and provisions, sent to ministers' families in Alabama, Georgia, New Mexico, and Oklahoma; boxes of supplies for the DePeyster Home, the Harward Home, the Berkeley Home, another in Mississippi, and, beginning in 1918, the Binghamton Home. Self-denial envelopes were used as early as 1914. From 1924 to 1928, a Miss Malone's tuition expenses were paid at the Washington Training School. Subjects for the group's study included Chinatown, Indians, Mormons, and Puerto Rico. There was also a Young Women's Auxiliary or Queen Esther's Circle, which actively explored such topics as immigration, child labor, and race relations. They used mite boxes and sent money for thank offerings, and help to medical missions and homes.

FIRST CHURCH, ENDICOTT, reports a Women's Home Missionary Society was organized in 1911, and a Queen Esther Circle started in 1921.

The SMITH HILL Women's Home Missionary Society was organized on May 7, 1922, with sixteen members paying one dollar yearly dues. They sent fruit and vegetables to the Children's Home. This work was later adopted by the Epworth League.

UNADILLA sent money to the Deaconess Home in Binghamton, reporting that the Home now has fourteen children, with much more room needed. There was plenty of space available for building, but no money to build. Unadilla also sent money to Brooklyn Hospital and to Aiken Hall, Olive Hill, Kentucky.

ONEONTA DISTRICT: The first annual meeting of the ONEONTA DISTRICT Home Missionary Society was convened in Unadilla, New York, on June 2, 1910, with Mrs. Priest as President. An interesting paper was read by Grace Peckham, Bainbridge, on the South Land. Other reports also were made:

> BAINBRIDGE reported organization of a children's group.
>
> At the second annual meeting in Sidney, four Vice-Presidents were elected, as a result of dividing Oneonta District into four groups.
>
> Every District meeting spent a great deal of time with devotions and singing. There was usually a guest speaker, to bring information about the work of the W. H. M. S. Puerto Rico was of concern, as were the poor of the deep South, the immigrants, the Children's Home, the Deaconess Home in Binghamton, and deaconess work elsewhere.
>
> In 1914, a report told of the National Soldier's Home and Hospital in Washington, D. C., where there were 1,200 old soldiers living in the Home. At age seventy, soldiers would be put into the Hospital for active care. The report noted that all of the nurses at the Hospital were Catholics, and asked the Society to do something to represent Protestantism. A committee was appointed to study the matter.
>
> At another annual meeting, a paper was given on "The Swinging Gate," and new light was shed on personal responsibility of all Americans toward newly-arrived immigrants.
>
> In 1915, the desire of the Deaconesses to established a Children's Home in Binghamton was discussed; by 1916, a report told of a Children's Home being established in Johnson City for Wyoming Conference.
>
> A report on Mormonism was given at another meeting, with the plea that efforts be made to combat this fast-growing sect, and that legal means be used to outlaw Mormonism's existence.
>
> A later meeting established a fund, with seventy dollars, to bring home the body of the Rev. George Benedict, Oneonta District's first missionary to Puerto Rico, to fulfill his desire to be buried beside his wife. Records show this was done.
>
> Many familiar names are in these minutes: Mrs. Hickok and Mrs. Finch, ministers' wives; VanCott, Unadilla; Wilde, Mount Upton; Peckham, Bainbridge; Tuller, Norwich; Case, Russell, Hall, Clark, Carr, from Sidney. Mrs. A. L. Weeden and Mrs James Hare seem to have been favorites for duets.

During the sixty years of the Women's Home Missionary Society, an efficient organization of women changed the lives of thousands of people. Over a quarter million women were members of the national organization, with an income of a half-million dollars, and assets of ten and one-half million. Wyoming Conference pledged to the national Society, during the last year of its separate existence, $15,675.

The W. H. M. S., having proven its worth and realizing that women's organizations all had the same goal—"A Better World, A Christian World"—was convinced that one cooperating women's society could surely achieve more, with less work, expense, and time, than a number of separate groups. Millions of women, working together with God's guidance, could change a suffering world, to one of peace and justice.

4.   Ladies Aid

The Ladies Aid, or Ladies Aid Circles, of the Methodist Episcopal Church were first formed on September 1, 1873. Their object and aim were: "... to promote, as far as possible, the financial and social interests of the church. To unite the women of the church and congregation in good works, and organize their labors systematically for the glory of God and the good of mankind."

At BETHANY, PENNSYLVANIA, they organized on September 22, 1893, as Ladies Aid, and in January, 1897, they renamed the organization as "What So Ever Society." At a meeting two years later, though, they were persuaded to change the name back to Ladies Aid. In 1899, they raised one hundred dollars toward the erection of a new parsonage. Dues were ten cents per meeting. They paid $5.00 per month toward the minister's salary, and taxes as follows: For the parsonage, county tax, $3.00; school, $1.20; poor tax, $3.00; borough tax, $1.50. Total taxes per year amounted to $8.70. On February 24, 1926, they paid the assessment of $48.00 for the Children's Home. In May, 1930, a hall was acquired, with the Society paying $300.00. They raised $8.00 toward the minister's salary of $75.00. In 1933, forty active members were listed.

DURYEA, PENNSYLVANIA, organized July 12, 1919. They still have the same Constitution and By-Laws, committing themselves as follows:

1. To maintain the Christian faith and promote the observance of the services and the ordinances of the church.
2. To assist the Pastor in parochial work.
3. To assist the Official Board in advancing the temporal interests of the church.
4. To endeavor to induce others to attend church by visiting strangers, encouraging sociability, making arrangements for entertainment and receptions and thus afford means of improvement and recreation under the control of religious influences.

The Constitution contained ten Articles and ten By-Laws. Article II reads:

> A woman of good moral character wishing to avail herself of the privileges and benefits of this church shall be eligible for membership by paying ten cents per month and signing the Constitution.

In 1925, they were paying $75.00 as their portion of the pastor's salary. Their minutes, from July 12, 1919, to November, 1940, are preserved in two large notebooks.

WESTFORD, NEW YORK: Records are not available, but older people remembered the Ladies Aid long before 1924: the money-raising efforts, the quilting bees, oyster suppers, and the very-popular ice cream socials. A local farmer harvested ice for the ladies' use for the almost-weekly summer socials, which were apparently one of the most popular fund-raising projects of the church. The Ladies Aid helped to pay the minister's salary and the janitor's compensation, and helped to care for the parsonage. In 1933, they voted to call themselves "The Willing Workers," but Rev. Adams, arriving that year, advised them to remain Ladies Aid, as were other Methodist women.

COOPERSTOWN: According to records from the 1913 Centennial history by Mrs. Rogers, the Ladies Aid existed for many years, but its beginnings are lost. At one time, it was known as the "Mite Society," because members were fined five cents for various things, the money going into the mite box. In 1892, there were twenty-four members. In 1897, the Constitution and By-Laws were adopted, and, in the same year, they raised $500.00 for repairs to the Elm Street Church. Meetings usually followed Prayer Meetings. When the present church was built, the ladies contributed $700.00.

VESTAL CENTER: On June 23, 1885, a meeting of ladies was called, to discuss repairs to the church. The group later organized as a Ladies Aid Society. Funds were raised by the women, and in 1894, Brother Jenkins was appointed, in cooperation with the ladies, to purchase glass for the windows. The Ladies Aid presented a bell in 1897.

SOUTH STERLING was chartered on a Friday the thirteenth, 1893, with thirteen (apparently not superstitious) initiating members.

LA ANNA was chartered in 1895. The first bazaar and supper were held in a shed a half mile from where the church was to be built. The ladies worked very hard to help raise the money for the building. The church was dedicated in 1899.

FRANKLIN FORKS was organized September 8, 1880, for the purpose of helping to furnish the church. In 1883, they spent one hundred dollars for pew cushions, which action they later regretted, as the cushions became quite lumpy. After this purchase, they had only fifty-five cents in the treasury. Carpeting was purchased for the church for $99.75; later, in 1939, carpeting was again purchased from Sission's in Binghamton, for $199.14. By way of contrast, carpet bought in 1960 cost $1,400.00.

LEHMAN, PENNSYLVANIA: The church was built in 1856. A Ladies Aid Society was the first organized group in the church, meeting in homes for worship and planning ways to serve the church. They made quilts and did all types of handiwork, in addition to sponsoring dinners and teas. The ladies were divided into two divisions, taking turns with the responsibility of money-making projects and serving. In 1938, they served a delicious Christmas dinner for $.25 per person, and exchanged ten-cent gifts.

The NORTH GHENT Ladies Aid Society was formed in 1880, the same year that church was built. In 1881, they paid ten dollars to help liquidate a church debt of $33.89. They met monthly, with a dinner including the menfolk. Their records burned in 1955.

DAMASCUS, PENNSYLVANIA: The first mention of a women's society here was made in minutes from 1863. There was much opposition, but they did continue, as Ladies Aid, until 1930, when they changed their name to "The Methodist Guild."

UNIONDALE: In 1882, the ladies were expected to buy any furniture needed for the parsonage and serve dinners once a month, charging $.25 for adults and $.10 for children.

NANTICOKE, NEWPORT, AND ALDEN, PENNSYLVANIA: Ladies Aid organized in 1882, known as Friendship Circle from 1920 to 1940.

SIMPSON CHURCH: From 1869 to 1926, the group was organized for the purpose of raising money by dues, quilting, and holding suppers, to purchase furniture for the church and parsonage.

CONKLIN FORKS: In 1880, the men of the church found it difficult to carry out all the duties expected of them, and so a Ladies Aid group was formed that same year. The women met monthly, bringing quilt pieces or cloth and yarn. Quilts were pieced and tied. They might be given to the minister, or put in the mission box. Clothing was repaired, and children's clothing sometimes made. A dinner was served at noon, with the hostess generally serving the main dish. The dinner cost ten cents per person; men were welcomed. At least once a year, the ladies met at the parsonage to help the minister's wife clean house. They washed windows, woodwork, and cupboards, sometimes papering a room or two.

Sometimes a missionary box was packed with clothing and toys to send to some mission field. The supply committee took care of mission work. If there was a wood bee, or threshing, or filling a silo, the Ladies Aid would help with the dinner, and a collection or donation was taken to add to their treasury. The biggest event of the year was the Fourth of July Homecoming Dinner. They usually served 100 to 150 people. There was no water, except what was brought in milk cans. The chickens were donated live and had to be killed and dressed, to be cooked later over a wood stove. A large sack of flour was usually required for the biscuits. After the dinner, a baseball game was played, between Conklin Forks and Hawleyton.

GREENE had no Society other than Ladies Aid. These women were divided into three circles, each responsible for four months' financial projects. They paid the organist ten dollars per month in 1924. They bought new dishes, four and a half dozen of each kind of dish, for $56.76. They tied quilts for $1.25. They bought a double-oven stove, a hot water heater, and a sink. The old minutes do not mention any mission pledge. The Ladies Aid did pay into the Entertainment Fund and made regular pledges to the Official Board.

MARATHON, NEW YORK: In 1897, the women of Marathon organized as the Ladies Union. They financed improvements to the church and parsonage, paying for lights, gas, and water.

SIDNEY, NEW YORK: The Ladies Aid reported having $205.05 cash on hand on April 15, 1905. They met monthly, raised money through suppers, bazaars, and other means, to undergird the church's financial support.

PORT CRANE was organized February 21, 1905. The church needed much assistance in paying the pastor's salary and buying needed items for the church.

MAINE was organized February 9, 1892, to help build a new church. The edifice was constructed in 1894, after which the Ladies Aid continued to raise money for church expenses.

FAIRDALE—from 1899 to 1940. The first women's organization was the Women's Christian Temperance Union, which later became a Ladies Aid Society. The women helped with the upkeep of the church and sent money for World Service and Near East relief, continuing to help pay the pastor. They seem to have been one organization long before the 1940 unification. They state that they built the parsonage with a good carpenter and $3,500.00. The parsonage is still standing in 1983.

DALTON: Copied from the minutes, 1885-1890: Organized 1885. 1885—paid to have the organ tuned. 1889—paid the church heating bill and hired a man to clean the church for fifteen dollars per month. 1889—assumed a debt of $150.00 toward furnishing the dining room and kitchen. Paid $20.00 for cutting a door. 1890—In December, they served a dinner to 98 people, for $.25 each. The last entry in this minutes book states: "See what a few have accomplished in less than five years."

SOUTH STERLING (PENNSYLVANIA), DAVENPORT (NEW YORK), UNION DALE, SMITH HILL, HONESDALE, THROOP, APALACHIN, MEHOOPANY, WYALUSING, MOOSIC, WORCESTER (NEW YORK), WEST PITTSTON (PENNSYLVANIA) all had active Ladies Aid Societies, all remembering the purpose for which they were organized, and accomplishing their goals in much the same manner: suppers, bazaars, and quilting, helping to pay the ministers and sometimes the janitors, and supplying various needs of the church and parsonage.

To all who have contributed stories and anecdotes about the work of women's groups within the Wyoming Conference, a debt of gratitude is owed; for these memories are, in a very real sense, the foundation for understanding the significant role women have played through the Conference's history.

END NOTES

1. Leroy E. Bugbee, *He Holds the Stars in His Hands* (Wyoming Conference, 1952), p. 199.
2. *Ibid.*, p. 201.
3. *Ibid.*, pp. 208-209, *passim.*

General Note: Much of the factual material for this article comes from Bugbee's (above) Chapter VII, "Women in Christian Service." Other materials were provided by individual respondents, members of women's groups within the Wyoming Annual Conference.

INTERVIEWS WITH TWO RETIRED CLERGY
OF WYOMING CONFERENCE

1. Leon W. Bouton, interviewed by George Hunsberger, January 11, 1983:

GEORGE HUNSBERGER: Leon, would you give us an outline of your personal history in the pastorate and in the Conference?

LEON BOUTON: Thank you, yes I was born to Webster Marvin Bouton and Bernice Carrier Bouton on 3 September 1905, in the Mount Vision parsonage on the Oneonta District, New York. My father was a member of the Wyoming Conference for 39 years. I was completely involved in the Furman Street Church, Syracuse, in my teens, until my college graduation. They gave me a license to preach on 3 September 1924. I was appointed student supply pastor by Central New York Conference to Lock Borough, New York, on the Geneva District, in 1926. I then went to seminary, and I was a student assistant at Copley Methodist Church, Boston, for one year; then I went on trial in the Wyoming Conference in 1928. I was student assistant and full-time associate in Wakefield, Massachusetts, for two years; I became a full member of the Conference and was ordained elder in 1930; and my first appointment was in Nichols and Lounsberry, New York, 1931, for two years. I was Pastor at Oxford and Guilford in the Oneonta District, 1933 to 1936; then, I was Pastor at Oxford from 1936 to 1938. We came to Fairview Methodist Church in Binghamton, 1938 to 1945, seven years; then to Carbondale Methodist Church, 1945 to 1947; First, Endicott, 1947 to 1958. I became superintendent, 1958 through 1964, appointed by Bishop Corson.

HUNSBERGER: What District?

BOUTON: Wilkes-Barre District. I came back to Ogden Methodist Church, Binghamton, in 1964, and stayed there until 1970, when I retired. I was close enough at the time. Later, I became interim pastor in the United Church of Christ twice, a Methodist once, and I became assistant to the pastor of First Church, Endicott, 1968 to 1971.

I married Emma Grace Fish of Delmar, New York, in 1930; she died in 1980. We have three children: Mary Wilson, Rev. David, and Rev. William Bouton.

I led the Conference in buying Sky Lake Camp in 1947, as the President of the Conference Board of Education. I was Vice-Chairperson of the Conference Board of Ministry for some years, and a director of youth camps. I was Conference Secretary from 1949 to 1952. I was Chairperson of World Service and Finance for two quadrenniums, beginning in 1973. I was a delegate to General and Jurisdictional Conferences in 1964 and 1966. I was a clergy member of the Board of Lay Activities in 1964 and 1968.

We bought our home in Endwell in 1973.

HUNSBERGER: Leon, think a minute about your membership in the General Conference. Do you have any reflections, at this point, on what you saw and heard there?

BOUTON: I enjoyed the General Conference very much, but I think General Conference is too big and does not last long enough. Many good things are lost in the present system, because of the size. I think the more representative Jurisdictional Conference should precede the General Conference, weeding out the non-essentials, and bringing to the General Conference specific proposals from the grass roots of the church.

HUNSBERGER: Leon, who, or what, influenced you to go into the ministry, and who is the most responsible in making this call successful?

BOUTON: When I was sixteen years old, I had an inner realization of the personal invitation of Jesus Christ, in a mid-winter Epworth League Institute, to go into the pastorate, and the Central New York Conference Session for Youth that year. The influences on my life in my pastorate are the influences of my Lord, my mother, my father, and the Rev. Herbert Downey, pastor of my church in Syracuse.

HUNSBERGER: There have been changes, no doubt, that you have noticed in the Conference. What are some of these, and, as you see them, which were productive, and which might have been unproductive?

BOUTON: When I joined the Conference in 1928, I understood the aims and goals of the Wyoming Conference were to recruit adults and youth as committed Christians. We emphasized Sunday School, youth work, and World Service giving. It seems that our Conference now invites commitment casually, ignores the follow-up of its recruits, gets excited over social issues, leaves youth to fend for themselves, downplays the Church School, spends a great energy in doing good by excessive organizations. It does not make much impact on modern issues, or modern members.

HUNSBERGER: Leon, what changes in Conference structure have been productive or unproductive, as you see it?

BOUTON: The Conference structure is an elitist group of sincerely dedicated leaders, spreading itself too thinly, quite unproductive, and slow in the turmoil of today in the needs of the people.

HUNSBERGER: Leon, you may have touched on it, but in your experience, what is the essence of Methodism?

BOUTON: The essence of Methodism to me is a warm, happy, conscious, experiential commitment to God and to life where the people live, plus intensive application of the gospel of Jesus Christ to the present issues of the local community first, and the world of the future.

HUNSBERGER: In the years that you have been in the ministry, have you noticed any change in the preaching, for better or for worse?

BOUTON: I think preaching has suffered from the lack of study, lack of personal relationships with the people, and too much time and energy in running organizations. When I began my ministry, we could point to a multitude of giants in the pulpit. Where are they now?

HUNSBERGER: And how has the emphasis on laity improved the Methodist Church?

BOUTON: The emphasis on the laity has improved the Methodist Church by releasing pastors to study more, to do more intensive work with persons, by testing the commitment of the laity to Christ and to expanding the influence of the church in local communities.

HUNSBERGER: You mentioned your family earlier. Did your family help you in fulfilling your ministry?

BOUTON: My honest opinion is that my family has been my most effective sermon. By exemplifying sacrificial service, sympathy for the needful, unity among ourselves in the home, desire for growth, good clean fun, and loyalty to an invisible world, my family has been my strongest support.

HUNSBERGER: Changing the trend a bit, what do you feel are the three greatest issues before the church now, and what were they as you began your work?

BOUTON: The issues when I began my work seemed to be denominational competition and hostility, graded Sunday School lessons, and alcoholism. Now, they are still alcoholism, the world arms race, the publicity of the gay community, suicide, confusion of youth about life-style, youthful crime, and personal holiness among Christians.

HUNSBERGER: Another question: How would you characterize your theology and changes in this theology?

BOUTON: As far as my theology is concerned, I hate being labeled. I began as a conservative literalist. My philosophy became personalist, and I have always tended to be post-millenial, if you like that. My theology has abandoned literalism, but it is still somewhat conservative, mainly liberal, influenced by liberation theology.

HUNSBERGER: Your were a superintendent for a period of time. What reflections do you have on that experience?

BOUTON: I enjoyed the superintendency a great deal. It put me in touch with the most capable people in the local churches. Of course, I had some administrative problems, but I was thrilled with the strength of the small churches. I think the superintendent should be selected, not on the basis of seniority, or big churches, but on a special aptitude in evangelism and counseling. The superintendent should be the pastor of the pastors. Superintendents should spend more time in private sessions with pastors and their families in their homes. Superintendents should have their own district programs, growing out of the local Councils on Ministry. They should have an eight-year term and stay with it the whole time.

HUNSBERGER: Leon, you were connected with the Dimock Camp. What reflections do you have now, about Dimock Camp and the campground?

BOUTON: The camp grounds of the Wyoming Conference were projects of the District Superintendents. The Dimock Camp Ground is 106 years old this year, and is as productive as the families with the children who take hold of a long-range program. I was president for one year. I had a great deal of enjoyment in it. The services now are more entertaining than challenging of the spiritual life by strong preaching, and small group sharing. Dimock Camp Meeting's strong quality is in its ecumenical nature and dedicated cottagers.

HUNSBERGER: Leon, think about your ministry. What legacy would you like to leave to the church of the future?

BOUTON: I would like to leave to the church a group of changed young men and women, with the best education, a definite call, an unselfish personality; with a great deal of *shalom.*

HUNSBERGER: We thank you very much, Leon. I'm sure that your recollections today have brought back many interesting memories of your years in ministry.

2.   Harry E. Brooks, interviewed by Robert W. Harris, November 3, 1982.

(The Rev. Mr. Brooks served Plymouth, 1912-1914; Smyrna, 1914-1917; Windsor, 1917-1919; Morris, 1919-1922; Milford, 1922-1927; Afton, 1927-1930; Susquehanna, 1930-1937; Nichols, 1937-1939; Vestal, 1939-1943; Newark Valley, 1943-1944; Bainbridge, 1944-1947; Chenango Bridge, 1947-1949; Waymart, 1949-1953; Court Street, West Park, Scranton, 1953-1963; retired, 1963. Following retirement, Mr. Brooks has been Assistant at Elm Park, Scranton, 1963-1965; supply at Hop Bottom, 1965-1966, and Throop, 1966-1970; and Associate at Asbury, Scranton, 1970-1974.)

HARRY BROOKS: With pleasure, I cooperate with this Conference Committee, in preparation for the observance of the Wyoming Conference celebration of the Bicentennial of American Methodism.

ROBERT HARRIS: We wish to ask you several questions, one of which is, Why did you enter ministry?

BROOKS: Why did I answer the ministry? Not of my own choice. I had hoped, when an adolescent, to prepare for mission work in India, where my cousin, Aden Paul Brooks, served for over twenty years as a teacher of chemistry at Allahabad Agricultural Institute. However, economic circumstances prevented my academic preparation for this ministry. In 1911, when I was twenty years of age, I was invited by the Rev. Ransom Floyd Lesch, pastor of my grandmother's church in Smyrna, New York, to consider the pastoral ministry, promising he would aid me in every way possible. I accepted this suggestion as a call from our Lord, and began my preparation. The next year, while in my studies, now having a local preacher's license, I was appointed to the Plymouth, New York, Methodist Church, as a supply pastor. I felt deeply the call to the ministry, immediately after Pastor Lesch invited me. I gave my heart to our Lord Jesus Christ and experienced the new birth at the age of eleven, in Brooklyn, New York, during a series of evangelistic meetings under the leadership of the famous John Davis, founder of the Practical Bible Training School of Johnson City, New York.

HARRIS: During your sixty-nine years in the pastorate, you must have some memories that stand out above others. Would you like to share them with us?

BROOKS: Thank you, Brother Harris, with gladness. Very briefly, these were: (1) The occasions of my ordinations as deacon and elder; (2) Visiting parishioners in a rowboat, during the Susquehanna River flooding of the 1930's; (3) My fifteen annual visits to the New York State Senate and Assembly, to act as Chaplain; (4) My two visits to the United States Senate and House of Representatives, in Washington, D. C., also to act as Chaplain; (5) My aiding President Harry Truman to compose the Thanksgiving Proclamation, by inserting a call to national prayer on one occasion of his presidency; (6) The visits of Bishops Chitumbar of India and McDowell to our church in Susquehanna, Pennsylvania, to address a two-District meeting held there; and (7) My eight preaching missions in Europe, in fifteen different countries, all glory to our Lord.

HARRIS: Having been, myself, on an exchange to England, I am most interested in your preaching missions in different European countries. What similarities and differences do you note between American United Methodist Churches, and Methodist Churches abroad?

BROOKS: Very briefly, may I note these? First, the accelerated tempo of the American Methodist Church, its programs and business methods. Second, the seemingly larger emphasis on the "spiritual" in European churches, and the more extensive use of laypersons in leadership in England's churches.

HARRIS: Would you like to comment further on lay leadership in English churches?

BROOKS: Well, it seems to me that the lay leadership in England is so pronounced, that in many places, they take the roles of ordained ministers. In fact, most of the churches of England, at present, are served by laity. We have a scarcity of ordained clergy in England, and consequently the utter dependence upon the laity.

HARRIS: Would you agree with something else I noticed while there, namely, that the laity take their offices very seriously and engage in pastoral visitations and in other things, aside from Sunday preaching, that we might associate exclusively with ordained clergy?

BROOKS: It is absolutely true, Brother Harris, and I feel that the leading part taken by laypeople in the work of the Methodist Church in

England is one of their outstanding and characteristic views. I commend the use of laypersons in the English Methodist Church.

HARRIS: Amen. What are the most significant changes you have noticed in the church during your ministry?

BROOKS: Well, Brother Harris, there are many, only a few of which I would mention. First, of course, the methods of transportation for the pastor went from horse and buggy to automobile. I drove a horse in serving my churches for twelve years, before I gave in to driving a car. Secondly, the dropping of the Prayer Meeting in weekly session, is, to me, very sad. Thank God there are some churches in our Wyoming Conference who are yet conducting weekly Prayer Meetings. Again, the decline of pastoral calling, and its inestimable benefits in the gathering in of new members and personal cultivation of the spiritual life of parishioners. And, following this, the change of Annual Conference entertainment, from being lodged in private homes, to housing in the University of Scranton dormitories; also, the movement of Conference sessions from churches to University facilities.

HARRIS: One of your major activities through the years has been with the Children's Home and the Homes for the Aging. Would you tell us some of the story of your involvement with these organizations?

BROOKS: Brother Bob, with great pleasure I do this, but very briefly. When I took my first charge, the little group of children cared for by our church was housed by our deaconesses in their Binghamton residence. My first visit to the children in an actual home setting, was in the farm house by the side of the road in Hillcrest. I was a member of the Finance Committee in the early days of the Home. As I recall, our first budget was $7,500, in utter distinction from the quite larger budget of today. I have kept in close touch with our Home through the years and am yet a member of the Board—honorary. Regarding the Homes for the Aging, for about eight years I pleaded on the floor of Conference for consideration of this great need, but with little tangible result. Finally, patience and persistence won, and the Conference authorized the committee to purchase the Moffatt Home on North Washington Avenue, for a very modest price for such a beautiful house. Before moving into this Scranton residence, I called upon Brother Roy Williams, who then was pastor of Asbury Methodist Church, to help me. We went to the North Washington Avenue residence, not yet occupied by people, having only recently been vacated by the Moffatts. We went from attic to cellar and had prayer in every room, imploring the divine blessing. Today, with six homes, and a value of more than twenty million dollars, these homes are serving scores of residents and offering future service to our entire Conference territory.

HARRIS: One other thing we would like to ask is, Who influenced you the most during your years of ministry?

BROOKS: Brother Bob, I am very deeply moved by this question. You know, I could name so many people. I'll mention four, two clergy, and two laypersons. (1) Dr. Levi L. Sprague, of Wyoming Seminary, most famous and agreeable and genial soul, President of Seminary for many years; (2) Pastor Ransom Floyd Lesch, of this Conference, who invited me into the ministry; and (3) Two laypersons, Mr. and Mrs. Ziba Tuttle, of the Smyrna Charge, who took us under their wing when we first entered the ministry and gave us inspiration in their hilltop farm home for many years. They are now in heaven. We remember them with appreciation.

HARRIS: One question we would like to ask everybody that we interview is, What do you think the most important word or idea you could leave to the future would be?

BROOKS: Thank you, Brother Harris. They are multiple, rather than singular: (1) Study; (2) Pray; (3) Read the Scriptures regularly; (4) Read great brain-teasing books; (5) Call on your parishioners.

HARRIS: Thank you very much.

General Note: These two conversations are part of a series of similar interviews, conducted by the Wyoming Conference Commission on Archives and History as a means of preserving the memories of earlier times. This Oral History Project seeks the bygone days of the Conference, as recollected by persons who helped to shape these events. The interviews with Leon Bouton and Harry Brooks have been transcribed, with some editorial correction, from taped recordings.

SWORDS AND PLOWSHARES:
WYOMING RESPONDS TO WAR

William W. Reid

In 1972, the Wyoming Conference Board of Christian Social Concerns presented a resolution dealing with amnesty for those who left the country or went to prison rather than participate in the Vietnam conflict. It said in part:

> Among those who have conscientiously objected to participation in war are thousands of young Americans who are in exile in Canada and hundreds more in Sweden or other countries, in addition to many hundreds in American civilian and military prisons. The church has a major responsibility to initiate or join efforts to secure amnesty for these and others who have resisted war by violating selective service regulations, or civil or military law in connection therewith.

The Scranton Tribune reported, "The proposal triggered an immediate debate with nearly a dozen clergymen and laymen taking the floor to air their opinions."[1]

The proposal was defeated 118-84, and a substitute motion was adopted:

> We support those individuals who conscientiously oppose all war, or any particular war, and who therefore refuse to serve in the armed forces. We also support those persons who conscientiously choose to serve in the armed forces or to accept alternate service. Pastors are called upon to be available for counseling with all youth who face conscription, including those who conscientiously refuse to cooperate with a selective service system.[2]

One layman was furious. "My son is in Vietnam," he said to his pastor. "He is risking his life, while a bunch of cowards run off to hide. I hope that we can discuss this in Sunday School after my boy gets back home."

The pastor agreed, and in due time the layman's son returned. The following Sunday, amnesty, as it had been discussed at Conference, was related to the dozen members of the adult class. The father said, "Before others say what they think, I want my son to speak. He's been to Vietnam and knows what's really going on."

Much to the father's amazement, his son replied, "Amnesty is a good idea. I don't have any problem with fellows who went to Canada. Some of them have been saying things that need to be said, and it took courage. After all, we're trying to protect the right of people to disagree and to say what they think."

As one seeks to understand the response of the Wyoming Conference to social issues, it may seem that the Conference has moved with singleness of mind and spirit. Often, however, as these disagreements at Annual Conference and in the Sunday School class demonstrate, there has been a diversity of opinion and deep struggles, as the people called United Methodists in this area have wrestled with the issues of the day.

In this paper we shall attempt to see a part of the struggle and the changing outlooks as we observe the response of the Conference to the wars in which the United States has been involved.

CIVIL WAR

In 1857, when the young Wyoming Conference made its first official statement regarding slavery, it did so with two convictions: the righteousness of the cause and the possibility of a peaceful resolution of the conflict.

> During the present generation the Discipline has steadily rung in our ears the great moral question, "What shall be done for the extirpation of the evil of slavery?" This fact implies that, as a church, we regard slavery a great evil—that the means of its extirpation are human—that the church should ever seek its removal; and that her agency is peculiarly appropriate to the case. That slavery is powerful, and that efforts for its removal are exciting and difficult is admitted. . . . The supposed pecuniary interest of our countrymen in the support and extension of Slavery—the lust of pride and personal power—the balance of political control between the North and the South—together with the habits and education of slaveholders, render this one of the most difficult subjects of moral reformation ever investigated. . . . Yet, . . . the extirpation of Slavery is deemed perfectly practicable . . . Slavery must not advance, but recede. It must not be extended, but extirpated. The moral part of this work is ours. The M. E. Church must furnish . . . the necessary moral power for such work. . . . It would be a disastrous shame to her to leave it in this land to be accomplished by either Mars or Mammon . . .[3]

In 1860, the Wyoming Conference, in its resolution, "On Slavery," said that:

> real slaveholders have no right in the Church of God, where the great Head of the Church admits of no respect of persons; and where . . . men-stealers are classed in moral turpitude with liars, murderers of parents, man-slayers, and perjured persons.

The Conference called upon the 1860 General Conference to "make provision for the exclusion of all such real slaveholders as shall refuse to manumit their slaves." In an apparent reference to the Methodist Episcopal Church, South, the Conference also stated,

> We strongly desire that the Church to which we belong shall never have the least appearance of being compromised on this subject . . . by affiliating with or recognizing the Christian character of any other body of men upholding slavery.[4]

When the 1861 session of the Wyoming Conference began on April 11, members were well aware that the Confederate States of America had been set up by seven states on February 8th, with Jefferson Davis as president. When, on April 16th, they took up the slavery issue, they probably knew that Fort Sumter in Charleston, S. C., had been fired upon on April 12th; and they may have known that it had been captured on the 14th. The members of Conference were unwilling to accept the Report on Slavery, or a Minority Report on Slavery, or even to adopt again the report of the previous year. Finally, the Rev. B. W. Gorham presented the following motion which was adopted by a nearly unanimous vote:

> *Whereas,* Providence has taken the work of emancipation into its own hands, therefore,
> *Resolved,* That we stand still and see the salvation of God.[5]

In April, 1862, with the war a year old, a sober Annual Conference reflected on the rightness of the Union cause and the essential evil of the slavery position, took cognizance of the great suffering which that evil had caused, and, thanking God for victories won, asked for His continued blessing:

> We regard loyalty to a government like ours, fostered by God's own hand . . . as a duty so plain that argument in its support is superfluous . . .
> It is with the deepest sorrow and mortification we behold our . . . country drenched in blood, brought on for the overthrow of our government by the enemies of order and liberty. The hundred thousand lives sacrificed, the anxieties, mourning, and suffering which accompany and follow the waging of the deadly strife, and the thousand millions of property either destroyed or devoted to the support of the conflict, are all but inadequate signs of the terrible moral evils which originated and attend the present war . . . We devoutly render thanks to Almighty God for victories won . . . and we most humbly implore the continuance of his counsels, his support, and his blessing in aid of our holy cause as necessary to its success.[6]

When the members of Conference assembled in Carbondale on April 12, 1865, they knew that Lee had surrendered at Appomattox Court House three days before and that the Civil War, "the bloodiest war known in modern times," was about over. When the report "On the State of the Country" was presented on the 15th, it was not yet known by the Conference that Lincoln, whom they called "the second Washington," had been shot the night before and died that morning.

In reading the report, one is aware of many feelings of the Conference: joy, mixed with relief, and without signs of gloating; a sense that slavery was over, not only in America, but throughout the civilized world; a feeling that the great sacrifices were not too great, since the Union was preserved; a belief that democratic self-government would spread; and a feeling that moderation toward the Southern people, though not their leaders, was the path for the nation to take. The hand of God was seen in the victory; the war was His way of ending slavery; the loyalty of the preachers in supporting the cause (evidently using Romans 13 extensively) was seen as helping to turn the scale to victory; and slavery was denounced in terms of the evil powers of Revelation.

> The rejoicings of the present hour spring from that love of country which God has implanted in the bosoms of all. As a Conference, we can but feel how different the condition . . . now and four years ago . . . At our session then the earth shook, and the air was lurid by the bombardment of Sumter. Now we hear but the retreating echoes of the last great battle of the war. Petersburg is ours; Richmond is ours; and the boasted army of Virginia, with the Commander-in-chief of all the rebel forces, is ours; and glory, peace, Union, liberty are the fruits. . . .
> We have seen the end of slavery in our country, and *that* will end the abomination in the civilized world. And what is most remarkable about this, and shows most clearly the hand of Providence, is the fact, that while the North were looking in vain for some means to abolish slavery, the South have accomplished it by themselves; and that, too, by means of a rebellion commenced for just the opposite purpose. . . .

Though . . . the nation has waded in blood, and endured an exceeding weight of suffering, yet too great a price has not been paid; for in preserving the Union of these States, we have preserved everything that was politically dear to us; and, in losing it, all would have been lost. . . .

At a time when monarchs and aristocrats were predicting the downfall of our republic, and the failure of democracy in the earth, we have established, beyond question . . . man's capacity for self-government, by such a conspicuous triumph as will strengthen the cause of constitutional liberty everywhere. And though monarchies may still exist in Europe, despotisms cannot; and there will now be a stronger and more rapid march towards representative government in all the enlightened nations than ever before . . .

It is a time, too, which calls for moderation on the part of the victors towards the vanquished. And while the archtraitors should be held to rigid responsibility for their crimes, a Christian lenity should characterize our treatment of the Southern people; partly because they have been cajoled or forced into rebellion, and partly in view of the tremendous retribution which, in the providence of God, is now resting upon them. . . .

The pulpit . . . has been called to utter no uncertain language, but to reiterate the words of the great Apostle, that we be subject to, and heartily sustain those powers which are a terror to evil-doers and a praise to them that do well; that we recognize with ardent gratitude the noble stand which our ministers, in the main, have taken, in denouncing so fearlessly this wicked and treasonous rebellion, and its equally wicked cause; and that their efforts to educate, quicken, and give tone to the public conscience upon the stirring issues of the day, have had no small influence in turning the scale in favor of loyalty . . .

We recognize . . . the downfall of that system of human oppression known as American Slavery, which the sainted founder of our holy Methodism denounced "the vilest which ever saw the sun." Babylon, the mother of harlets and abominations is fallen! is fallen! Gog and Magog are thoroughly routed! No more slave-pens! No more slave-auctions! No more clanking of chains in a free country! The glorious doctrine of our immortal Declaration of Independence is fast becoming a living practical reality throughout all our land: "All men are created equal, and endowed by their Creator with certain inalienable (sic) rights, among which are life, liberty, and the pursuit of happiness."[7]

Before the 1865 Conference ended, word was received of the assassination of President Lincoln. A special service was addressed by Dr. George Peck, and a "Supplementary Report on State of the Country" said in part:

In the sudden and painful death of our Chief Magistrate, ABRAHAM LINCOLN, the nation has sustained an irreparable loss, forasmuch as he whom the people delighted to honor the second time to that office was, in our judgment, eminently suited to the responsible post, and has so conducted the affairs of the State during these troublous times as not only to inspire our hearts with the highest confidence in his honesty, but also in his statesmanship.[8]

That peace did not come easily, and that the divisions between North and South were deep, were recognized in 1868 and in 1879:

The spirit of that rebellion still lives to interrupt our peace, and retard our commercial, industrial, educational, moral and religious interests.[9]

We deplore sectional strife, and the widening and the deepening of the bloody chasm, made more and more sanguinary by the Confederate leaders who are endeavoring to gain the lost cause by sweeping away Constitutional guards and destroying laws most wholesome . . . While we are seeking fraternity with our Southern brethren, and sending contributions to their sick and suffering, we protest against the sword, crimson with the blood of our brethren, being waved in our faces.[10]

The response to the Spanish-American War was far different from that to the Civil War for a variety of reasons: it was short and decisive, with few casualties; it was against another nation from which few Americans had come; and our nation was catapulted into the position of a world power, this being seen as part of God's design for our people.

Meeting in April, 1898, just a few days before the beginning of the Spanish-American War, the Wyoming Conference took note that war might be very near. Reciting the misdeeds of Spain, including cruel treatment of the Cuban people and the sinking of the "Maine," the Conference adopted a report which said,

> We are convinced that no satisfactory and abiding peace for Cuba can be reasonably expected short of the absolute and permanent withdrawal of Spain as a governing power from that island. We believe that this result should be attained by peaceable measures if possible, but if not, by the exercise of force as a last resort.[11]

In 1899, with the war with Spain a matter of history, but with a guerilla war against insurgents being fought in the Philippines (a struggle which would continue until 1901), the Conference debated the issue:

> The Committee on the State of the Country presented its report . . . J. A. Faulkner spoke on the report and offered an amendment to strike out of the report all reference to our policy as a nation in the Philippine Islands.[12]

The report at this point was returned to the committee, which later presented it in an amended form which was adopted. It said in part:

> The last report to this body . . . ended with the prayer "That the conflict may be short and decisive."
>
> . . . God in His providence has gloriously answered the prayer. Three hundred years of Spanish misrule in Cuba and Puerto Rico have come to an end . . . The shortness and decisiveness of the conflict that made these people free, took away the breath of the nations, and opened the eyes of the world to the resources, the skill, the celerity of movement, the phenomenal heroism, the overawing majesty of sixty millions of people . . . whose providential mission is to proclaim, "Liberty throughout the world."
>
> It is a matter of rational and grateful pride, that the glory of our arms, on sea and land, shines with a lustre, that pales not its brightness side by side with the most illustrious deeds of human heroism and achievement, and that the names of Dewey and Schley, with that of the immortal Nelson, will burn in the splendor of bright particular stars, in the heartfelt admiration of men, till the heavens are no more. . . .
>
> Deploring deeply the loss of our brave men in the contest now going on in the Philippines, we yet put the strongest emphasis of approbation on the policy of our government in regard to them.[13]

The sense that the Spanish-American War was a part of God's plan and God's doing was expressed strongly by the Conference in 1900.

> Our Monroe Doctrine outlined the Western Continent as our "Sphere of Influence," not to dominate our weak neighbors . . . but to encourage and defend them. The logical converse of this doctrine was the implied promise of non-interference in other parts of the world. *But,* Divine Providence would not have it so. And, therefore, without our seeing subsequent steps, He called our nation to arms in defense of the suffering Cubans. A holier motive did not move St. Paul to gird up his loins and pass over into Europe to

answer the Macedonian cry, than drew this whole nation together as one personality to undertake for our neighbors. God gave Manila into the hands of Dewey. He must hold it till Spain's Philippine possessions were ours. And then, lest we should selfishly retire and leave the field of labor to which He had called, He allowed the misguided Tagalogs to pour out the blood of American soldiers. And so, from the beginning of the Spanish-American war we have been led along step by step, Providentially, and *compelled,* unless we would be inconsistent or cowardly, to assume and hold a strong position as one of "The World Powers."[14]

WORLD WAR I

Western civilization entered the twentieth century with the belief that the age of reason and the age of science had come; no longer were the powers of darkness and ignorance in control; war was considered a thing of the past. That World War I could take place was deemed highly improbable; that such a war could happen between so-called enlightened Christian nations bordered on the impossible. That it happened was a blow to humanity's self-image. The only explanation was that it had to be the war to end wars.

The Wyoming Conference journals of 1915 and 1916 reflect none of this struggle. There is no indication that a war was going on anywhere. As far as the printed record is concerned, it was business as usual. By the time of the 1917 Annual Conference, all had changed.

On April 6, 1917, some two months after breaking off diplomatic relations with Germany, the United States declared War and entered World War I. Five days later, on April 11th, the Wyoming Conference convened in Cooperstown, N. Y. Patriotic feelings ran high, and members quickly noted a display of the flags of the United States and of her allies. John A. Faulkner presented a resolution which was adopted by a rising vote:

> We desire to acknowledge with gratitude and appreciation the action of the pastor and those kind friends who have placed our own flag and the ensigns of other powers which represent with us the principles of liberty, as symbols both of our national patriotism and of that international fellowship which must be the next step to secure world-peace.[15]

That same afternoon, "On motion of John B. Sweet the Conference decided to adjourn immediately following the ordination of Harry C. Fraser, in order to participate in the farewell parade to the departing volunteers, and that in so doing we carry the American flag."[16]

Three days later a resolution by Hugh C. McDermott was adopted:

> Whereas, The Methodist Episcopal Church has ever been zealously loyal to the Flag, esteeming the love of country and second only to the love of God; therefore be it
>
> Resolved that we direct all our pastors to have our Nation's Flag conspicuously displayed in all our churches and Sunday School rooms during the period of the present war.[17]

At the session on April 16th, the Journal states, "Oscar L. Severson, holding aloft our Country's Flag, in a most enthusiastic patriotic address, presented the following report on behalf of the Committee on the State of the Country:

When the Conference of 1918 convened in Wilkes-Barre, members were
informed at the first session "that the Evening News has consented to furnish
the Conference with the latest war bulletins."[19] A Committee on Patriotic Expression was appointed, with John H. Race as chairman. The committee's
report said in part:

> As loyal Americans we count it a privilege to sacrifice in order that just and fraternal
> relationships among men and nations shall be established. The task of civilization is the
> task of all. We must win this war. . . .
> Our immediate duty . . . is to do our part in the mobilization of the communities
> represented by us as a Conference as to bring the importance of this task to the attention
> of all within the sphere of our influence. Even the civilian must not lose sight of that fact
> that though his service in this present crisis is less dramatic than that of the soldier in the
> trenches, nevertheless the civilian has a task that is full of daring and sacrifice.[20]

The 1918 Conference Journal set a "first" for the Wyoming Conference
with a cover in color as it portrayed the American flag in red, white and blue.
(For some reason, the flag on the cover was a 45-star flag, even though the
48th star had been added in 1912.)

The gloating about national power which followed the Spanish-
American War was not reflected in the 1919 Journal. Instead, there was a
reflective 6-page report on "The State of the Church," written by George P.
Eckman, which addressed such things as the task of the Church, the response
of the Church to the war, and dangers and opportunities facing the Church
in the post-war era.

> (With so many persons killed or wounded), the ministry of consolation is the first
> order of service for the Church of the compassionate Christ.
> A practical Church will . . . retain . . . and utilize the altruistic impulses and the
> sacrificial devotion of (persons who volunteered for philanthropic service).
> An alert Church will discern in (the passion to make the war a triumph of right) an
> intimation of what is possible . . . when the deepest springs of moral action are touched
> by a sufficiently asserting motive.

Eckman described what happened in the Church and on the battlefields:

> The regular processes of religion were jarred . . . Pulpits were transformed into
> rostrums for instruction and agitation respecting the moral aims of the war and the duty
> . . . to further them. The preacher who clung to the traditional business of proclaiming
> dogmas . . . saw himself gradually deprived of a constituency, while he who thundered
> against the Teutonic diabolism found himself the center of an increasing circle of the
> pious and the patriotic.
> God came to be expressed not in terms of philosophical and theological precision,
> but in terms of social order, of international justice, or even of military necessity. He was
> under compulsion of His very character to give victory to the defenders of liberty. Men in
> the trenches used grotesque familiarity with the Deity. They prayed one moment and
> cursed the next, and to them their petitions had equal propriety. Our pulpits showed
> scarcely greater discrimination. In the fury of a just indignation they hurled thunderbolts
> hot with vengeance. They claimed divine approval for their fiery denunciations, and

evidently it was granted; for the skulking poltroons of Prussia, abandoned of the criminal coward in whose name they fought, sank into helpless confusion . . .

Conditions were cited which were "in certain respects prejudicial to the interests of religion." Among them were:

> A sudden reversion from tense anxiety to intense joy . . . (which has) deluged most of our people with its mad hilarity. It is perhaps a natural and inevitable reaction, but its current sets away from God . . .

> A recrudescence of national pride, begotten of a triumph to which America contributed in a critical hour of need, but for which she suffered little in comparison with England, France and Belgium. The braggart spirit which prompts vulgar speakers and writers to affirm our ability to whip the whole creation whenever the occasion may arise, a tawdry and ignoble boast in which even some good but misguided Americans indulge, tends strongly to pull us away from God and to focus our reliance upon ourselves and our possessions.

> A swift return to money-making and money-spending as the chief ends of living . . . does not carry us toward God.

> Industrial revolt and social insurrection . . . When monarchs lose their crowns by assault it is an easy suggestion that whatever is up should come down, and that whatever is abased should be exalted. Even God is threatened by the agitators of this frenzied upheaval.

Several "Advantages Resulting From the War" were lifted up:

> New sense of duty . . . a responsibility for others, world-wide in extent, and eternal in its depth and durability.

> Reinforced conviction of the solidarity of mankind. The herosim of the Hindu, the Chinaman, the African, the barbarian, rivalled that of the Anglo-Saxon, and surpassed that of the Teuton and the Turk. No man can henceforth be despised for his race, his color or his condition. Caste has received its death-wound. The whole world is kin.

> New determination that the earth shall be made decent and kept so . . . that never again shall it be the plaything of creatures called monarchs, whom the accident of birth has lifted to an eminence their merits could not win.

> New consciouness of God . . . as . . . a person who has unveiled Himself in loving comradeship in prisons foul and fields of blood. An awareness of God's presence in His own world, in which He has not lost his way, but will maintain His sovereignty, until all wrongs are righted and all kingdoms merged into . . . the kingdom of righteousness.

> An understanding of the Cross such as no generation ever had before. The central truth of the gospel has become the pivitol fact of history. Our boys have no dogmatic explanation of the atonement, but they know the significance of the just dying for the unjust. They being strong have borne the infirmities of the weak, and like the Son of Man they have found it their joy not to be ministered unto, but to minister and to give their lives a ransom for many. A hundred thousand pulpits and thrice a hundred thousand Bible classes could not have taught these lessons half so effectively as the Lord has imparted them through the ordeal of a world war. God is the supreme strategist and has seized His opportunity with infinite wisdom and skill.

If the demands of the hour were to be met and peace were to be won, it was necessary "that religion . . . lay hands of authority on every area of human activity." Two things were required: that the Churches work together, and do so with holiness of character. "It was the lack of these which made it impossible for the Church to prevent the war. The absence of these will render the Church incompetent for its present task. Protestantism must speak with the authority of unanimity." In a vision which was not to be captured, the report said,

The cultivation of a true spirit of internationalism is largely a function of the Church in the name and by the power of Jesus Christ, the world's first democrat. Our fathers fought for independence; our sons have been fighting for interdependence . . . The nations of the earth bust (sic = must) be organized into a fraternity. No patriotism finds a Christian level till it passes beyond the interests of a single country to the welfare of universal humanity. It may be idealism to seek a league of nations to maintain peace, but the dream of Jesus includes the unity of all lands under the scepter of love.[21]

Thus the Conference gave its blessing to the concept of a league of nations for the keeping of the peace; but it did nothing more officially in support of such a development. Aside from prohibition and the observance of the Sabbath, no social issues were addressed until 1928.

In 1928, Leon K. William presented a report for the World Peace and Social Service Committee, which protested war as a national policy and looked askance upon military parades.

We must stand for the outlawing of war as being the arch-crime, and the advocacy of a world court. And we must remonstrate against policies that stage provocative parades of armed forces. . . .[22]

The 1930 report, presented by Dr. Henry H. Crane, noted that the disillusionment following the war "has manifested itself . . . in the sense of depression or even skepticism with reference to social idealism, the widespread tendency to turn religious aspiration and moral passion into individualistic channels, often at the total exclusion of all important social issues . . ." It added:

Any practice or program . . . that tends to prepare for war we definitely renounce. This country is committed to peace. With over half a hundred other nations we have definitely renounced war as an instrument for the settlement of any dispute or difference, Why then should we continue to prepare for war by maintaining large military machines, carrying on military training in public or private schools and by direct and indirect means aid the development of the military mind?[23]

WORLD WAR II

As World War II approached, and even after it began in Europe, the Conference outlook was a blend of pacifism and isolationism.

On April 5, 1940, the Wyoming Conference convened in Athens, Pa. Britain, France, Germany and Russia were already at war. Poland had been overrun; Finland, stubborn and proud, had succumbed to Russia. In four days, Norway and Denmark would be invaded; and in another month, France and the Lowlands would face the full fury of the Nazi attack. The World Peace and Social Service Report reflected the mood of many in those times:

We believe that war is an expression of the evil in man and not the good and we believe that Christians must refuse to have a part in it . . .[24]

In 1941, the same committee asked

members of the Conference to lead their people into calm sanity in the presence of a situation within which national passions may be aroused.[25]

Two weeks after the fall of Bataan on April 8, 1942, the Conference met in session in Wilkes-Barre. The Social Service Report quoted from a statement of the 1940 General Conference:

> The Methodist Church, although making no attempt to bind the consciences of its individual members, will not officially endorse, support or participate in war. We insist that the agencies of the church shall not be used in preparation for war, but in the promulgation of peace. We insist that the buildings of the church dedicated to the worship of God shall be used for that holy purpose, and not by any agency for the promotion of war. We heartily suggest that our churches offer their facilities for every possible humane ministry in connection with this emergency. It should remain The Church, supra-national, world wide, keeping inviolable the fellowship of devout believers in every land. It is the one unbroken fellowship throughout the world. This mutual love exists even in this hour among sincere Christians of Japan, Germany, England, France, Poland, Australia, India, the United States and all other countries on earth. Church members should pray always for their enemies as themselves.[26]

The District Superintendents, in their composite report presented to the same session of Conference, said:

> The American people will support the nation's war effort to the end, but the Christian Church is concerned about something beyond the defeat of the enemy. She is concerned about the preservation and conservation of human values and Christian ideals. When this conflict ends, when the last gun has been fired, the last ship sunk, the last bomb dropped, what then? The Church is pleading for the healing of the nations and for a new order in international and human relations in which the moral law of God shall be obeyed and in which there shall be a world wide willingness to live in fellowship in the spirit of Jesus Christ.[27]

In 1943, the Conference called for "the establishment within each Church of study groups for the considering of the problems and bases of a lasting peace." Churches needed to face the issue of

> The preparation of the mind and motives of church members for the establishment of a just and enduring peace—a peace without blood purges, reprisals or the annihilation of former enemies, a peace founded on economic justice, international law and the practice of interracial brotherhood dedicated to the ideals of the Sermon on the Mount.

The churches were alerted to "a world-wide self-righteous nationalism which threatens the establishment of any international order based on the ideals of Jesus."[28]

The 1945 session of Conference began on April 11th, a day before the death of President Roosevelt. On April 13, the Conference held a memorial service and sent telegrams to Mrs. Roosevelt and President Truman. The Social Service and World Peace Committee called for "the study and support of the Dumbarton Oaks proposals, as the first step toward world order."[29]

In 1946, the Conference sensed that peace would not come easily or quickly.

> The Christian Church stands at the threshold of what may be the twenty-five most perilous years in world history. A second world war has ended, leaving unchanged every major tension with which it began.

Churches were urged to respond to the famine which "stalks half the earth;" and the President and Congressional representatives were urged to:

Abolish *compulsory* military training of any type.

Abolish the policy of military isolationism by pledging any moral use of force to the United Nations for the purposes of international police protection.

Withdraw American occupation forces as quickly as possible from all areas where the civilian government is strong enough to control the situation.[30]

KOREAN WAR

The Korean War received little mention in Conference procedings. The only direct reference was in the 1951 report of the Co-ordinating Committee on Social Action:

> The making of an honorable peace through negotiations is not a sign of weakness; therefore let there be a "cease-fire" in Korea and peaceful solutions sought through the United Nations.[31]

In 1952, the Conference approved a report of the World Peace Committee which did not refer directly to Korea but which said in part:

> It is our task to create the will to peace, the conditions of peace, and the organization for peace. . . .
>
> The Church . . . must use its spiritual power to destroy war. We see that our only earthly security is in obedience to God . . . We see the task of the Church as that of reconciliation, of healing, of the removal of hate and prejudice, the cementing of the bonds of brotherhood, and the proclaiming of Jesus Christ as the Saviour of us all.[32]

The day after this report was adopted, the Executive Session of Conference adopted the minority report of the Conference Board of Ministerial Training and Qualifications and discontinued Richard Fichter, who was seeking full Conference membership. Some apparently felt that, because his Mexican wife (the daughter of a Methodist minister in Mexico) could speak little English, he would be hard to appoint to churches. But the chief argument against his Conference membership was his refusal, on Christian principle, to pay any income tax because it would help support the war effort. "He didn't obey the government; he shouldn't belong to the Conference," was the sentiment of many.

That night, Dr. Henry Hitt Crane of Central Methodist Church, Detroit, formerly pastor of Elm Park Church, Scranton, and a great prophetic voice in the Church, spoke at a Conference dinner honoring Henry R. Van Deusen of Elm Park, a long-time member of the Judicial Council. While Dr. Crane did not mention Dick Fichter by name, it was quite clear what he was talking about as he spoke of the need to take our stand with people who take unpopular stands in witness to their Christian faith. Many felt that if a second vote had been taken the next day, Fichter would have been admitted.

VIETNAM WAR

Unlike the other wars in which America has participated since the organization of the Wyoming Conference, the Vietnam War started with a gradual buildup over a period of years, rather than with a big bang. The first American involvement began on June 27, 1950 (the same day that American forces were sent to Korea in response to the North Korean invasion), when 35 military advisors were sent to Vietnam. After the French withdrew in 1954 and the Geneva Agreements divided the country, American buildup gradually increased. By the end of 1963, there were over 15,000 American troops in Vietnam; the build-up accelerated after August 7, 1964, when Congress passed the Tonkin Resolution in response to the reported attack on two American destroyers; and, by the end of 1965, there were 184,000 American troops in Vietnam, and the total finally reached 543,000 by April, 1969.

Beginning in 1965, the Conference Board of Christian Social Concerns began to raise the issue and call for church action.

> The worsening crisis in Viet Nam is certainly a matter of concern to the Christian Church . . . The purpose of the Church's participation in this area is to create an atmosphere where new and creative approaches may be made by our church, national and world leaders.[33]

> We are grateful to men of courage such as Sen. J. William Fulbright and others, who have stood before the country asking questions and voicing the doubts which many have about America's policy in the Far East.[34]

> We urge the U. S. government immediately to initiate necessary steps leading to the withdrawal of all its forces from Vietnam in a manner to be determined by negotiation.[35]

> The members of the Wyoming Annual Conference do hereby publicly record our continued agonizing over American involvement in the Vietnam conflict, and . . . urge the members of our churches to communicate with our President, Richard M. Nixon, requesting him to use the powers and influence of his office to effect a cease fire and negotiated settlement at the earliest possible moment.[36]

> We urge the government of the United States to extricate itself from all military intervention in South Asia as rapidly as possible . . . We call, also, for the active participation by the United States Government and voluntary agencies in promptly formulating adequate plans and procedures for reconstruction, preferably through multi-national channels; for every effort to renew and conserve the peculiar heritage of the Vietnamese people: for the provision of a major share in funding the re-development of the country.

> This conference . . . would encourage (involved national and international church groups) to continue to make representations to North Vietnamese diplomats abroad in a effort to ease the plight of (American prisoners) and their families. We urge that internationally accepted standards should be respected in the treatment of these prisoners even as such standards should also govern the treatment of prisoners taken by the Saigon government and the United States forces.[37]

RECENT PEACE ISSUES

Unfortunately, the Church's verbalization of the demands of the Gospel has consistently outdistanced the world's performance, and threats of war continue to plague the world. In 1981, as a part of the report of the Church and Society Committee, "Guy Burt addressed the Conference concerning the situation in El Salvador and the need for a non-military solution to their problems."[38]

As a part of the 1982 report, the threat of nuclear destruction was shown through the film, "War Without Winners;" and the Conference adopted a resolution on nuclear freeze, which said, in part,

> We endorse the Nuclear Freeze Petition, the Hatfield-Kennedy Resolution calling for a mutual U. S. — U. S. S. R. nuclear weapons freeze on further production or deploy-

ment of such weapons . . . (We) call upon all those nations having or developing nuclear weapons to renounce first strike or use of nuclear weapons as a matter of policy or as a military option; that . . . nations . . . renounce the so-called tactical nuclear weapons . . . (and) . . . begin negotiations aimed at reducing present nuclear arms levels with the goal of total nuclear disarmament, to be accompanied by redirection of resources towards peaceful projects for the development of health and welfare among needy people. . . .[39]

CONCLUDING REFLECTIONS

As one reads the various responses of the Church and the Conference to the wars in which our country has been involved, it becomes apparent that the attitudes of the Church, whether strong support or vacillation or opposition, have generally paralleled the attitudes of the country. The question is whether the Church reflected these attitudes, or helped to create them. To this writer it would seem that, while the Church has, at times, reflected the outlook of the country, in two wars at least—the Civil War and the Vietnam War—the Church helped to shape that outlook.

The Methodist Episcopal Church was in the forefront of those who opposed slavery and sought its elimination. The issue of emancipation, and the war which seemed necessary to support it, were seen as a holy cause. As the war dragged on, and many in the North were willing to let the South secede, in order that the conflict might cease, the M. E. Church continued to urge support of the war, realizing that secession would mean the continuation of slavery.

The election of 1864 put Lincoln against Gen. George McClellan, who wanted to end the war quickly by allowing the South to go its separate way. The Wyoming Conference openly expressed its joy at the re-election of Lincoln, who was committed to winning the war. Lincoln himself clearly stated his appreciation for the support of the M. E. Church;[40] but he was apparently not involved in the special favors shown to the M. E. Church by Secretary of War Edwin Stanton.[41] The support of the Church was apparently an important factor in creating the willingness to see the war through to its victorious conclusion.

The response of the Methodist Church was far different a century later when war raged in Southeast Asia. The Vietnam War was never a popular war, and many felt uncomfortable with the ever-increasing American participation in its escalation. Outright opposition, however, was slow in developing—perhaps because of confusion about American goals and because of the holdover of McCarthy attitudes, which questioned the patriotism of anyone who opposed military action against forces supported by Communists. When concerted opposition to the Vietnam War did arise, it found a large degree of support in the Church; and that opposition played a major part in the efforts to end the conflict.

The Wyoming Conference, together with most other religious bodies, jumped on the bandwagon in support of the Spanish-American War and World War I; God and country seemed to be traveling hand-in-hand, both in goals and methods. By 1919, however, George Eckman was wondering if some hadn't been too enthusiastic about the conflict and was pointing to the causes of war which needed to be corrected, were further conflicts to be avoided. One wonders to what degree he spoke for himself, and to what degree he reflected the attitude of the Conference.

Much of the pre-World War II sentiment of the Conference paralleled the isolationist mood of the country. In its official pronouncements, the Conference did not jump on the band-wagon in enthusiastic promotion of the war, though a large percentage of Methodists probably supported the war-effort as fully as non-Methodists. There were far more conscientious objectors in World War II than World War I; and their acceptance, though never very enthusiastic, was wider than in World War I. To what extent the statements of the Church and Conference affected this, is impossible to measure.

The actions of the 1952 session of the Wyoming Conference present an enigma. One day the Conference could say that "our only earthly security is in obedience to God;" and the next day it could reject for its ministry a man who sought to live in such obedience. This contradiction raises questions about our pronouncements and our actions. Are statements on war and peace, adopted by the Conference, really the reflection of a minority, rather than a majority, viewpoint? Are many in the Church willing to go along with rhetoric, but not with consistent action? Are there times when our minds can accept certain ideas, which get overthrown when they come in conflict with our feelings? How does the Church help people deal with the conflicts which so often arise between the goals of the nation and the goals of the Christ?

Where the future will lead us is still not clear. The present controversies over American involvement in Latin American struggles and over nuclear weapons capacities also place many in the Church in opposition to stated government policies. The degree to which the Church can or will influence ultimate decisions in these areas (or speak in judgment if not able to shape national policy) is a matter for which the outcome is, as yet, uncertain.

END NOTES

1. Scranton *Tribune*, June 3, 1972.
2. Wyoming Conference *Journal* (WCJ), 1972, pp. 132-133.
3. *WCJ*, 1857, p. 9.
4. *WCJ*, 1860, p. 21.
5. *WCJ*, 1861, p. 8
6. *WCJ*, 1862, pp. 33-34.
7. *WCJ*, 1865, pp. 10-11.
8. *WCJ*, 1865, p. 12.
9. *WCJ*, 1868, p. 19.
10. *WCJ*, 1879, p. 50.
11. *WCJ*, 1898, p. 110.
12. *WCJ*, 1899, p. 44.
13. *WCJ*, 1899, pp. 119-120.
14. *WCJ*, 1900, p. 129.

15. *WCJ*, 1917, p. 31.

16. *WCJ*, 1917, p. 35.

17. *WCJ*, 1917, p. 51.

18. *WCJ*, 1917, p. 56.

19. *WCJ*, 1918, p. 32.

20. *WCJ*, 1918, pp. 45-46.

21. *WCJ*, 1919, pp. 109-114.

22. *WCJ*, 1928, p. 127.

23. *WCJ*, 1930, p. 336.

24. *WCJ*, 1940, p. 756.

25. *WCJ*, 1941, p. 89.

26. *WCJ*, 1942, p. 323.

27. *WCJ*, 1942, p. 287.

28. *WCJ*, 1943, p. 544.

29. WCJ, 1945, p. 93. The groundwork for the United Nations was laid at the Dumbarton Oaks Conference in Washington, August - October, 1944 and brought into fruition at the United Nations Conference on International Organization which was convened in San Francisco on April 25, 1945, ten days after the close of Conference.

30. *WCJ*, 1946, p. 372.

31. *WCJ*, 1951, p. 724.

32. *WCJ*, 1952, pp. 1021-1022.

33. *WCJ*, 1965, p. 137.

34. *WCJ*, 1966, p. 172.

35. *WCJ*, 1967, p. 136.

36. *WCJ*, 1969, p. 153.

37. *WCJ*, 1970, pp. 146-147.

38. *WCJ*, 1981, p. 73.

39. *WCJ*, 1982, pp. 76-78.

40. The 1864 General Conference sent a committee to meet with President Lincoln to "assure him of the sympathy and fidelity of the M. E. Church, in the great struggle to maintain the government and to blot out the foul institution of slavery." Lincoln responded, "We would not utter what might in the least seem invidious, yet without doing this, we may say, that the M. E. Church, not less devoted than the best, is by reason of its numbers, the most important of all. God bless the Methodist Church—bless all the Churches, and blessed be God who giveth us the Churches!" Quoted in *WCJ*, 1876, p. 34.

41. "By an order of Secretary of War Stanton, November, 1862, at the suggestion of Bishop E. R. Ames, . . . Union commanders in the Departments of Missouri, Tennessee, and the Gulf . . . were instructed to place at the Bishop's disposal 'all houses of worship belonging to the Methodist Episcopal Church, South,' in which a loyal preacher 'appointed by a loyal Bishop . . . does not officiate.' " "When the orders of the military departments were brought to the attention of President Lincoln he wrote to Stanton expressing embarrassment at what had been done, particularly in view of earlier statements that he (the President) had made. 'I have never interfered,' he had written, 'nor thought of interfering as to who shall or who shall not preach in any Church, nor have I knowingly or believingly tolerated anyone else to so interfere by my authority.' " Quoted by Wade Crawford Bailey in *History of Methodist Missions* (The Board of Missions of The Methodist Church, New York, 1957), Volume Three, p. 302.